CW00968420

A Concise Guide to

NATURE PHOTOGRAPHY

Peter C. Harper

ROBERT HALE • LONDON

Dedication

Joan Wakelin

First published in Great Britain 1994

ISBN 0-7090-5476-9

Robert Hale Limited
Clerkenwell House
Clerkenwell Green
London EC1R OHT

Printed in Singapore

CONTENTS

Much has happened since my first book, *Photographing Nature*, was published by The Caxton Press in April 1989. Autofocus cameras have arrived and are now here for good. This book explores this new technology and discusses its advantages and its shortcomings for the nature photographer. Inevitably, some of the advice offered in my previous book – now out of print – has been retained because the 'new age' photographers still find it very helpful: for example, the problems of buying 'second hand' cameras and lenses and some practical approaches to light, picture composition and other important generalities.

In the 1990s autofocus rules supreme. Now a new breed of students inhabit our photography classes, demanding to know everything about these wondrous cameras. Again, the cry for a new book to save them writing tedious notes. So, here it is, freshly minted, with a new set of images.

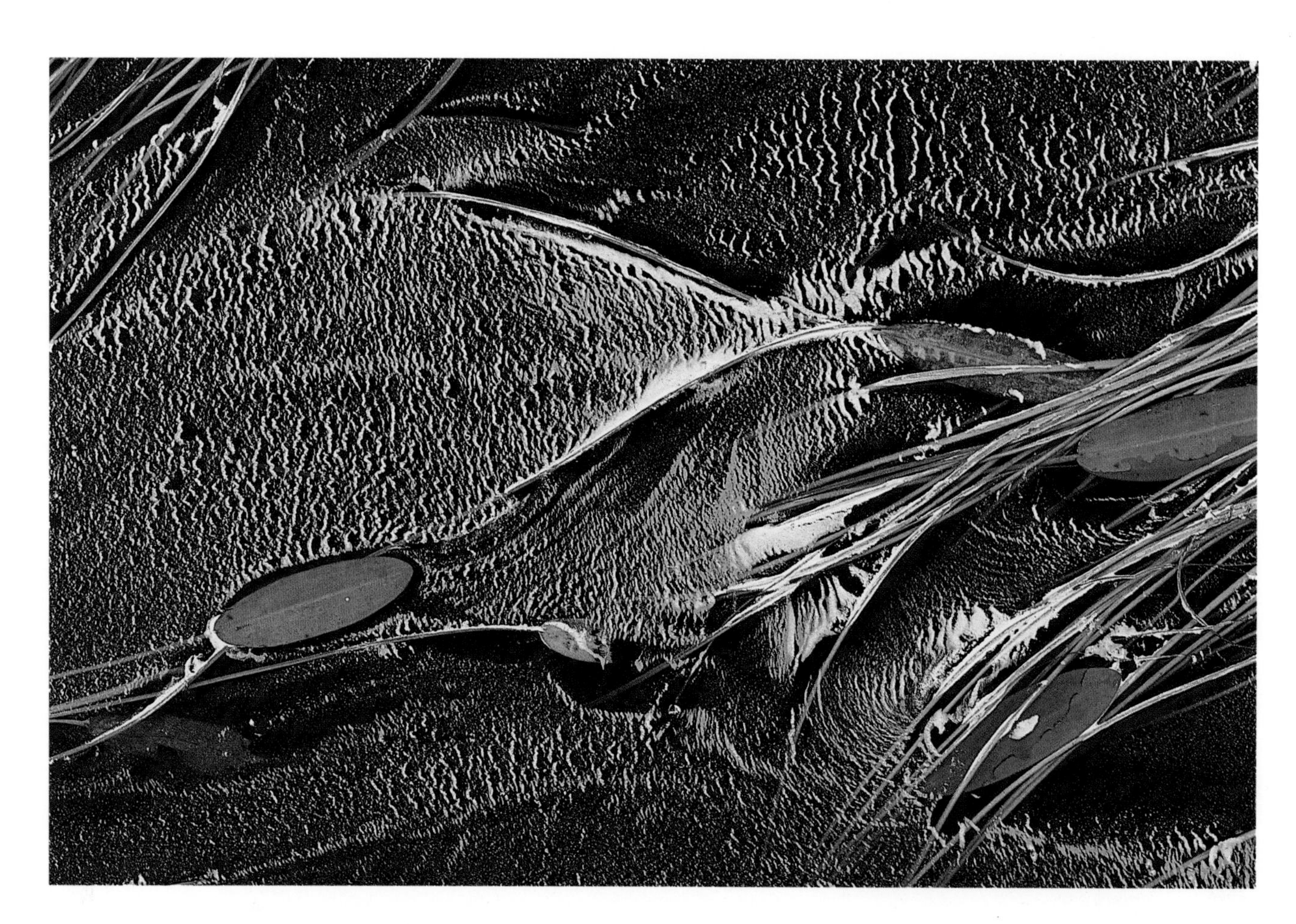

POND WEED SYMPHONY

Fuji Velvia 50 Canon EOS 5 with Canon 100 macro lens, f/8 at 1/30 sec. Tripod.
A still afternoon, a forest lake, pond weed, and a heavy dusting of yellow tree pollen, and here's what can happen. A small wharf provided a sound tripod support. Watch for bright reflections beaming off the water.
A polarising filter can help, but if you can change your camera position in relation to the sun, then try this first.

I am deeply indebted to my colleagues and friends for their advice, some of their work, and their time to help me write this book. In this regard, I especially want to thank Matheson Beaumont and Richard Poole. Former students Paul Kennedy and Stephen Wright read the text to ensure that I had explained things as clearly as I could.

Some of the better images in this book are not mine. They have been generously supplied by Matheson Beaumont, George Chance, Di Forbes, Lynn Hutton, Gary Jones, Paul Kennedy, Martin London, Jane MacLeod, Bruce Stead, and Bevan Tulett. My wife Lynda's images also figure large here too. Colin Monteath of Hedgehog House provided me with eight images from his photo bank. My thanks to Colin, Tui De Roy, and the other photographers for their excellent work.

I am especially grateful to Mike Armstrong and Ole Hansen of Canon New Zealand Ltd for supplying me with their excellent camera equipment during our 1992 study tour to Nepal, and for their support for my photographic requirements and our nature photography programme thereafter. Hugh Flaus of T.A. Macalisters Ltd has provided me with much information and support with Nikon cameras over the years. My thanks again for his help.

I use Fuji transparency film exclusively. My film requirements are sponsored by Hanimex (NZ) Ltd through Tim Steele, Manager of Fuji Professional Products. Hanafins ProLab (Lawry Hanafin, Manager) supplies my E6 film processing requirements, and do an excellent, professional job of processing it. I am deeply appreciative of this most important support. Thank-you Tim and Lawry.

Canada's Freeman Patterson and Britain's Joan Wakelin came to New Zealand for one of our photography weekend seminars in February 1993 and, while here, they kindly helped me sort most of the images for this book. My sincere thanks to them.

Andy Dennis of Nelson kindly edited the first draft of this book; Michael ffolliott-Foster, Executive Editor at The Caxton Press, edited the final version. My thanks to Michael and Bruce Bascand for, once again, keeping faith with me and my work. Jack Kempen designed this book and saw it through its production phases.

I stand on the shoulders of many clever and kind people. Thank-you everyone.

A SMALL LANDSCAPE

Fuji Velvia 50, Canon EOS 5 with Canon 100mm macro lens, f/16 at 1/8 sec. Tripod.

Landscapes are usually regarded as large vistas, but when you have a macro lens on your camera, and some interesting schist rocks to consider, think of small landscapes. They can be just as beautiful and full of texture and line as big ones. The view here is no more than 2 metres across.

FOREWORD

In the words of Edward Steichen, "The mission of photography is to explain man to man and each man to himself"

Whilst living in Sri Lanka, I learnt that teaching is the noblest of professions and photography as communication, its noblest calling. Images at their most passionate and truthful best, are as powerful as words will ever be.

The role of the photographer is to witness and be involved with the subject, to discover, to capture, to pluck feeling; to translate and make coherent, to preserve that frozen reality and make it breathe into a vital and living single moment. The role of the teacher is to develop in the student not only skill and expertise, so that technique becomes second nature, but an awareness of life about us, to encourage a personal and individual creativity. This voyage of discovery, this 'travelling hopefully', is one we as photographers/teachers share, and we have an enormous responsibility for keeping this enthusiasm alive. A photographer never 'arrives' and, with this philosophy, new and untrodden paths continue to reveal themselves.

Technical advances in cameras give the false impression that photography is just pressing a button - and its popularity continues to rise. The use of photography, and often its abuse without knowledge, can give rise to insipid and diluted imagery. In this book, Peter shares his expertise with an easy and direct style. It is packed full of information and I particularly like his anecdotes on personal problems solved and his helpful advice on many subjects, including travel. The pairing of his aesthetic, perceptive and gentle vision, with his technical skills, his teaching experience and the quality and purity of his images, make this book not only a hive of information but one which makes enjoyable reading. It is a MUST for those who have just got the 'bug' - and also for those who may need a refresher course.

It is with pleasure that I write a Foreword to Peter's book. I was delighted to pay a return visit to New Zealand, which is truly 'God's Own'. Thank you Peter, for sharing your involvement and deeply felt convictions, and for reminding us that, above all, photography is FUN.

Joan Wakelin, Hon. FRPS.

This book encourages you to become a better, more discerning photographer of nature. It's essentially a bag full of all sorts of handy hints and good ideas that I have found helpful for students over 13 years of teaching photography at the University of Canterbury.

The first chapter discusses photographic equipment. I have tried to make my comments relevant to most autofocus, single lens reflex cameras (hereafter referred to as AF cameras) available at the time of writing.

The following chapters will take you on a visual and written journey through designing a photograph and the allure of light - ideally to create in you a special way of seeing things, an ability to paint with light, and a willingness to detect natural patterns and textures in what you see. I next discuss landscapes, and then move from the expanse of wide horizons to those of the small. After Life in the Landscape there are chapters on Travel Photography and Close-up Photography, with the final chapter designed to help you with your Flash Photography.

BEACH ROCK
Fuji Velvia 50, Canon EOS 5 with Canon 100mm macro lens, f/16 at 1/15 sec. Tripod.
Soft sedimentary rocks moulded by the sea can create beautiful shapes for the photographer to work with. Add a spice of contrasting colour - here emerald green algae - and you have an image with interesting shapes, colour and texture. Rocky shores can provide the attentive photographer with a wealth of attractive options.

THE POHUTUKAWA TREES

Fuji Velvia 50. Canon EOS 5 with Canon 28-80mm L zoom lens. f/16 at 1/60 sec. Tripod.

By placing the sun directly behind the branches of a Pohutukawa tree I was able to set an attractive mood for this coastal scene. When shooting into the sun, remove all filters to prevent flare on your lens. I used no exposure compensation for this shot - a tribute to the modern camera's ability to cope with difficult lighting conditions.

Camera equipment is expensive, so it's best to do it right the first time. Here's a list to help you.

THE CAMERA BODY Buy a camera from a reputable manufacturer such as Canon, Minolta, Nikon, Olympus, and Pentax. These cameras are well made and reliable and have many useful accessories. Service and parts for these cameras are generally available, should they break down or be damaged. Avoid super buys of unfamiliar makes, and insist on a written guarantee with whatever you purchase.

Also avoid fully automatic cameras. Unless they have a manual override, such cameras have more control over you than you have over them. You must be able to operate your camera manually when the need arises.

THE AUTOFOCUS (AF) CAMERA

The autofocus camera represents a major advance in camera technology. Most manufacturers offer amateur and professional quality AF cameras with features that will greatly please nature photographers. Not all models have the items we need, so take time to choose your camera carefully. Here are some guidelines.

First, the good things about autofocus cameras.

Autofocus cameras use microcomputers to remove you from the technical problems associated with taking a photograph. Now it's all at your fingertips: autofocusing, power-winding, auto-bracketing: you name it.and it's ready for you. You can't even forget to put a film in the camera because it will beep at you and the window in the camera back will reveal all.

The key fact is this. **The autofocus camera allows you more time to consider why you are taking a photograph, rather than how you are going to do it.** Now you have more time to look carefully and to think of what you are doing.

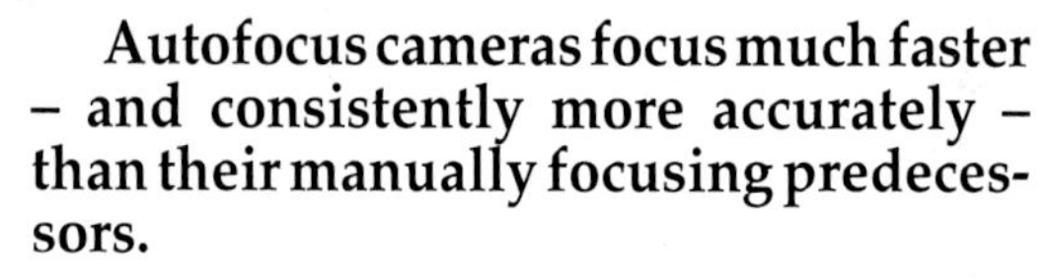

Autofocus cameras focus much faster – and consistently more accurately – than their manually focusing predecessors.

It's true. Precise electronics and small coreless motors can indeed outperform eyes and hands. AF lenses tend to be lighter in weight because the heavy manual helical focusing rings are no longer necessary. This has been somewhat offset by some professional cameras, themselves, being heavier, because of their need for battery power. As technology continues to gather pace, I would expect to see newer, fibreglass reinforced, polycarbonate camera bodies becoming stronger and lighter, whilst at the same time, lens designs will become brighter and lighter too.

Modern lens makers are now putting tiny ultrasonic motors in close contact with the focusing section of the lens, thus producing impressive speed of focusing and the torque required for starting and stopping focusing extremely quickly. Wildlife photographers will now find their monster AF telephoto lenses produce sharp images as quickly and easily as the smaller lenses. And with focus-tracking these lenses make photographing a bird in flight an absolute breeze. Probably the greatest triumph for autofocusing is ability to snap big telephoto lenses instantly into focus.

In poor light autofocus lenses can focus on objects that we can barely see.

This is a boon for nature photographers seeking a subject in deep shadow. No more squinting and fogging up the eyepiece with frustration.

Autofocus cameras finally do away with those dreadful split image screens that have long plagued manual focusing cameras.

Three cheers for this! You might like to think about replacing the plain screen that comes with the AF camera body with a screen that has grid lines, both to help you get horizons straight as well as to assist with your composition. A grid screen is particularly helpful for vertical shots.

Some autofocus cameras offer cordless electronic cable releases. Now you can fire the camera from about three metres away using an infra-red remote. No cords. It's easy. Just make sure that you stand in a place so that the infra-red sensor in the camera can pick up the signal from your remote, otherwise the camera will not fire. And watch where you put the remote after you have taken your picture - particularly if you regularly lost your old standard cable releases. Now you can lose the much more expensive remote.

Future developments in AF cameras. What might we expect?

Stiff competition will produce all sorts of wonderful developments. Witness the Canon EOS 5 which uses 5 focus sensors and an ingenious infra-red-sensitive microchip to assess where you are looking in the viewfinder. Two infra-red beams reflect off your eye's pupil and cornea and these instructions are sent to the camera lens which autofocuses on to the activated sensor. An exciting, somewhat awesome development. A logical extension of this would be full autofocusing on anything within the frame that your eye focuses on. So, in future, you might have to watch out if you have had an extra glass of ale before setting out with your camera.

Nikon have been busy, too. The Nikon F90 allows you to programme the camera exactly the way you like it. If you are shooting a subject that requires you to deviate from your favourite camera settings, all you need to do is push a reset button and everything is returned to your customised settings. Very handy. And how about your instruction book and photographic tips being stored on a palm-sized electronic organiser which you can carry around with you? Expect more nifty developments in the near future.

Some cautions about autofocus cameras

Take care when inserting the batteries

Do it right, do it with care. Some cameras will wink their delayed action light at you when you get it right. Get it wrong and nothing will move. Make sure the terminals are clean and free of grease. Mark each battery with the date that you put it in your camera.

Don't forget to turn your camera off after use

If you don't it can be totally brain dead when you need it next time. Some cameras will automatically shut down most functions to conserve battery power, but few actually turn themselves off. A camera with a fresh battery, left on overnight, can be totally useless by morning.

Where you and the camera want to focus the lens on a specific subject may not, in fact, be the same place.

This can result in a tug-of-war between a distraught photographer overriding the camera's autofocusing motors by hand and brute force. Such conflicts can be truly terrifying to behold. The solution is to switch to manual focusing whenever you need to. AF lenses are very easy to focus, either by battery power, or manually. It's great to have the option of doing both.

Autofocus lenses sometimes cannot focus on a featureless surface that has no clearly discernible edge.

The lens will react to this by hunting in and out seeking something on which to focus, while the batteries go down and your temperature goes up. To avoid this find, if you can, a suitable substitute the same distance away and focus on it. Then, holding the focus lock button down, recompose your picture the way you want it and shoot. With a bit of practice this is quick and easy.

Telephoto autofocus lenses need careful aiming.

If you have a large telephoto lens on continuous autofocus, so that it's constantly altering the focus as a subject moves closer or further way, watch that you keep the autofocus sights firmly fixed on your subject. If the autofocus aims at the background beyond your subject, the lens will re-focus on this, and it may take some time to be redirected back on to your subject – which may have disappeared by the time your lens focus arrives on the scene.

Watch out for loss of autofocusing.

Always check to see that all your AF lenses focus properly, especially zoom lenses extended out to their maximum focal length. Manufacturers can make mistakes. One particular make of lens worked well at 75mm and up to about 210mm, but at 300mm the camera's autofocus module wasn't receiving enough light to do its job properly and the lens failed to autofocus! After I drew this to the attention of the wholesaler, the lens was swiftly withdrawn from sale, and a new, corrected model, soon appeared in its place. Nonetheless, there are still a few AF telephoto lenses available for sale that will not focus on any subject when the light is poor and when they are extended to their maximum focal length. They tend to be in the 75 to 300mm f/4.5 - f/5.6 focal length category. Check carefully if you are considering one of these zoom lenses.

Watch out for tele-extenders.

If you put a tele-extender on some relatively slow lenses, (particularly zoom lenses), there may not be enough light entering the lens for the autofocus module to focus the lens properly, and the lens will hunt in and out. Change to manual focusing.

If you do revert to manual focusing, don't forget to return the focusing control back to autofocus when you have finished with it. If you have not done this the lens will not autofocus when you require it to do so – Murphy's Law (if anything can go wrong, it will) will ensure that next time you will be wearing heavy gloves, and can't move the tiny lever when that fabulously rare bird flies overhead.

New batteries can expire well before you expect them to.

Particularly if you use either a big telephoto lens a lot, or take long macro exposures, both of which quickly burn through the battery power. Buy fresh batteries, recently made. Some have the date of manufacture stamped on their negative end. Label any new batteries with the date that you put them in your camera. You will be surprised how battery time flies when you're having fun.

Never leave home without a fresh set of spare batteries.

If you did this before you changed to an autofocus camera, you will never get away with it now. Murphy's Law again awaits you. If the worst comes to the worst, try warming your old batteries somewhere snug about your body. This helps, when your batteries want to die just as that miraculous sunrise begins, or you want to rewind a film and the batteries decide to call it a day when the rewinding film is still in mid-flight.

Some AF cameras powerwind the film fully into its canister. If you wish to change films half-way-through this can be a considerable nuisance. Those photographers with good manipulative skills can attempt the following. Engage the camera's rewind motor and meticulously watch the film exposure counter ticking its way back to zero. Just before it succeeds, snap the camera back open as the film counter reaches zero but hasn't had time to swallow the tail of the film. Try this using an old film to refine your technique. Refrain from any alcoholic beverages while so engaged. Newer cameras offer a specific programme that allows you to leave the leader of the film out of the canister. An excellent alternative!

Autofocus cameras and close-up photography

Because macro-photography requires critical attention to what's in front of and behind the line of focus, autofocusing is generally of little use for this sort of work. A good close-up photograph requires careful thought and some preliminary focusing, combined with frequent checks on the depth-of-field. Manual focusing is superior to autofocusing under these circumstances. In recognition of this, makers of macro lenses generally provide large, easy-to-use, manual focusing facilities. I manually focus all my macro images.

So much for the magical front end of your camera. Here's how the AF camera is programmed to take pictures.

Full Program

This essentially allows you to *point and shoot* at your subject. The camera does everything. It selects the shutter speed and sets the aperture setting to achieve specific results. For example, the Nikon F90 has a *Silhouette* Program (yes, this programme takes silhouettes of your subject), a *Hyperfocal* Program (one that maximises the amount of depth of field for increased overall sharpness), a *Landscape* Program, a *Sport* Program (emphasizes high shutter speeds and small depth of field) and a *Close-up* Program.

If you are a complete novice to modern photography, you will find taking pictures an absolute breeze with all this clever gadgetry at your fingertips. Nature photographers should, however, try to wean themselves off Full Program as soon as they can. The options below allow you to take a more active and creative part in your photography.

Aperture control priority

This allows you to set the aperture and the camera selects the appropriate shutter speed. Aperture control priority enables you to control what is to be rendered sharp on the film. This is most important for subjects such as landscapes and close-ups. Nearly all my images are taken on aperture priority.

Shutter priority

Camera shake is the bane of many beginners. Shutter priority avoids this by accurately determining the shutter speed, and by allowing the lightmeter to select the appropriate aperture setting. AF cameras have shutters which range steplessly from 30 seconds to about 10,000th of a second (i.e. if an exposure of exactly 1/139 of a second is required, that is what the shutter uses), and it is not always easy to determine the true speed of the shutter during exposure (for example, with aperture control priority cameras). Shutter priority eliminates the guesswork. Shutter priority also enables you to create special effects such as selecting a slow shutter speed – 1/30 or 1/60 of a second – and following moving objects and creating a blurred background as you do so. Or when you want to, to set the shutter at high speeds like 1/4000 or 1/12,000 of a second for stopping subjects in motion, or to minimise camera shake when using big telephoto lenses. You will need, however, very fast films to help you do this.

Manual control

You must have the ability to switch everything off and be totally creative when you want to. Manual control may not appear important to the beginner, but as you become more confident in your photography, there will be many times when you will want to do it your way, and not the way the camera tells you to.

Types of metering

How do AF cameras cope with analysing all the light levels in your picture? They use two or three methods.The first is *matrix/ segmented or full frame metering* where the

camera surveys all the light it can see within the frame and makes some ingen-ious decisions on the available light levels and what it thinks you want it to do next. If you are photographing snow, some AF cameras will automatically over-expose to give you the white snow you want and not the grey snow you might expect from most conventional cameras. This raises an important point. *It is essential that you become familiar with your camera's light-metering abilities as soon as you can.* Find out how smart it is, and how smart you need to be in order to use this facility to good purpose.

For example, suppose your camera automatically over-exposes to compensate for snow and then you come along and say 'I'll increase the exposure times by 2 stops to get white snow', the result will be then even more over-exposed! So, read your camera's instruction book carefully.

Centre-weighted metering reads the central part of the frame which is usually circumscribed by an etched circle on the focusing screen. Where your subject varies significantly from its background, you can use centre-weighted metering to obtain an accurate light reading. You can hold that reading, either by keeping the shutter release slightly depressed, or by pushing an exposure lock button which will be somewhere handy to your camera controls. Now re-frame the picture and take the shot with your subject nicely composed off to the side somewhere, but remaining correctly exposed. Centre-weighted metering provides an easy and essential solution for those images which have a high contrast between the light falling on the subject and the light illuminating the background.

Spot metering works meters off a small circle in the very centre of your screen: this allows for precise light readings of small or difficult subjects which are lost in a background of vastly different lighting conditions.

OTHER FUNCTIONS OF THE AF CAMERA

Depth-of-field preview button

This allows you to see what you have in focus in front of and behind your subject before you trip the shutter. *It is inadvisable to buy an AF camera without one.*

Some cameras such as the Canon EOS system offer an electronic means of determining depth-of-field. You first focus on the closest object that you wish to have sharply recorded on film and lightly push the release button. The camera records that distance as Dp 1. Now refocus on a distant place in your image that you wish to have sharply recorded in your photograph. Push the shutter release button lightly again for Dp 2. The camera will now record that distance, then simply re-frame and compose your picture and push the shutter release fully down. The camera computes the precise f/stop required to ensure that all you want is sharply recorded on the film and will take the picture according to your instructions. Great idea isn't it?

Exposure compensation control (+/-)

This innocent-looking control baffles many camera buffs. The ECC allows you to increase or decrease your exposure value by 2 to 5 f/stops on either side of the correct exposure as determined by your lightmeter. You are, in effect, overriding your lightmeter to achieve a different exposure from the one it thinks you ought to have. The ECC is normally calibrated in increments of either 1/3 or 1/2 of an f/stop so that small adjustments to the exposure can easily be made when required. It enables you to take a picture using the normal exposure, with the ECC set at zero, and then *bracket* that exposure by turning the ECC to -1 which will reduce the amount of light falling on your film by one stop. This will result in underexposure (the picture darkens). By turning the ECC to +1 or +2, we are increasing the amount of light falling on the film. This means over-exposure (the picture fades with increasing light). You will normally be provided with a visual warning inside the viewfinder when you are using the ECC. This is to prevent you forgetting to return it to zero after you have finished with it.

Note: You can reproduce the effects of the exposure compensation control by altering the film-speed rating, or by ignoring your lightmeter while you alter the shutter speed or f/stop. I prefer to avoid tampering with the film-speed setting however, because it is too easy to leave it set at the wrong place.

Delayed action release

This is useful for tripod photography when you've forgotten to bring your cable release. AF Cameras can be programmed to offer anything from 2 seconds to 30 seconds delay before firing the shutter, this is also useful if you have to run a long way to get into your picture.

Exposure lock button

Where the camera is using centre-weighted metering, an exposure lock button allows you to expose correctly a subject which might not necessarily be in the centre of the picture. If your subject is off centre in the photograph, you can take a lightmeter reading from it, lock that exposure with the exposure lock button, and then recompose the picture the way you want it. The result will be a correctly exposed subject.

Facility to change the focusing screen

Most quality AF cameras will allow you to remove the standard plain screen and replace it with a variety of other screen types. This can be useful as we shall see later.

Viewfinders

The majority of camera viewfinders only show about ninety-three per cent of the final image. The result is that you can get things around the edges of your slide that you thought you had cropped out during composition of the picture. Camera manufacturers justify this with the argument that by placing a slide in a slide mount, only about ninety-three per cent of the negative is left for you to view. But this is not always true.

Eyepieces

Cameras all have a viewfinder eyepiece which allows you to see what you're doing when looking into your camera. Some eyepieces unscrew so that you can replace them with a lens to suit your own particular optical needs. Which is great, except for one recurring problem – they frequently unscrew and get lost. Suddenly your camera's pentaprism and internal electronics are exposed to everything including dust, sand, rain, and your tears at missing that last great shot. My advice is to get an eyepiece that suits you and screw it in securely: bind it with a small dab of superglue. Simple, and it works.

Eyepiece correction lenses

If you wear glasses, you may find it difficult to see what you are doing at the best of times. Camera manufacturers make correction eyepieces which replace the ones fitted to your camera. These should be readily available at your camera stockist. Some cameras offer an adjustable diopter control which can be adjusted from time to time as your vision gracefully deteriorates with age.

Eyepiece shutters

Extremely valuable to nature photographers doing close-ups. An eyepiece shutter shuts down over the viewfinder eyepiece to prevent stray light coming in and disrupting the exposure reading. Most of the top-of-the-line cameras have them in-built, but many other cameras don't have them at all. A rear lens cap, as an alternative, will adequately do the job.

Dedicated 'through the lens' (TTL) flash

Taking good flash pictures is now made easy with microcomputers within the AF camera and its dedicated flash working together. This is one of the real advances in autofocus photography and the final chapter of this book (Flash Photography) has been devoted to it.

DX coding

All film cartridges have a bar code marked on them so that cameras can read what speed they are and set their lightmeter accordingly. Buy a camera that allows you to override DX coding and set any film to any speed you need. This is the only way you can push a film to a higher speed than that specified for it (see *Film* later in this chapter).

Non AF cameras

Yes, some are still made, such as the Contax and the venerable Leica. Ideal for craftsmen and craftswomen who still love the fragrance of well-polished wood, sun umbrellas on a hazy afternoon, and the smell of new leather. Yes, wonderful, but if your eyesight starts to fail . . . and focusing becomes a cuss . . .

Once you have your new camera

Never let the salesperson put a film in it. Listen to what they have to say and ask as many questions as you need, then take the camera home and learn everything about it before you put in the first film. Above all, *read the instruction book very carefully* – nothing is more important than this. AF cameras offer a wealth of options for you in order to improve your photography. Consequently such instruction books can be rather heavy going. But please persist with them. Try different ways of taking pictures until you have fully explored everything your camera can do.

Write the serial numbers of all your equipment in the back of your instruction book. Handy if you lose any of your gear.

FILM

Films are getting better and better, with finer grain-structure and increased contrast. All you need to do is find one or two films you like and stay with them. Don't flit from one film to another - it's a waste of the time you could be spending in getting to know a few films really well.

I always carry Fuji Velvia 50 ISO and Fujichrome Pro 100 ISO. I use the Velvia for close-ups, landscapes, and most things. When travelling, I'll take the Fuji 100 and push it to 200 ISO if the light is poor or the subject is speedy. Used in this way Fujichrome 100 is an excellent multi-purpose film, capable of producing quality results. Try it. Fuji and Kodak Ektachrome films use the E6 process and can be processed by most photographic laboratories in about two hours. Kodachrome 25 ISO is an excellent slide film which I used for many years until the new generation of improved E6 slide films tempted me away from it.

If you are just beginning photography, try a medium speed film such as Fujichrome 100 ISO. This film's speed will allow relatively fast shutter speeds in poor lighting. It will also allow you to explore your camera's facilities more easily than a slow film, which can be unforgiving to the uninitiated. Once your confidence grows, try other types of film. A 400 ISO film is a stop faster than 200 ISO which, in its turn, is a stop faster than 100 ISO. The difference between 25 ISO and 400 ISO film is 4 stops. Experiment to find the film you like. Remember that the best images usually result from slow films with fine grain. Remember, too, that ultra-fast film such as Ektachrome 1600/3200 ISO can produce very grainy results that can be unusually interesting.

Many people, including me, think that professional films are worth the extra money. Standard film is made within a +/- 1/3 stop faster or slower tolerance than its official ISO rating printed on the box. Now while this doesn't sound like much, it can get a bit tricky if the film on which you calibrated your meter was 1/3 of a stop fast, and you then go out and shoot a batch of film which might be 1/3 of a stop slow. The resultant cumulative discrepancy is 2/3rds of a stop – enough to give your images a sad look.

Professional films are manufactured to their precise ISO speeds as rated. If they're a bit fast or slightly slow this is written on the carton, or within the information sheet. With professional films you know exactly what you're getting.

Do not buy out-of-date film. All colour films comprise colour dyes which will change over time. Heat accelerates the process of deterioration, so make a habit of buying fresh film and storing it in your refrigerator at about 4 degrees C.

LENSES

The first step to creative photography is a discerning and selective choice of lenses. There are many to choose from – too many perhaps. Low dispersion glass and computer-designed optics and handling have all combined to produce some zoom lenses which are unquestionably superior in quality to many older lenses of fixed focal lengths.

One I well remember testing was a 24 - 40mm zoom lens which at full aperture (f/2.8) was superior in optical quality to a famous brand 24mm lens at f/11. The difference was decisive and plain to see.

So, after a lot of experimenting and testing of various makes and models, I have developed my personal short list. The following suggestions have worked well for my students, so here they are for you.

Canon 28-80L

Assuming that you enjoy general nature photography, you should begin with a short, wide-angle zoom. A 28 - 70mm f/2.8 AF is an excellent choice. Sharp, bright to see through (f/2.8 all the way from 28mm to 70mm) and easy to use. If you cannot afford your camera makers' lenses I recommend the cheaper Tokina ATX in this zooming range. The standard 28-70mm f/4.6 - f/5.6 AF lenses are smaller and cheaper, but they can be dark to see through in poor light.

Canon 20-35L

If you can afford one of the premium quality Canon or Nikon 20-35-mm f/2.8 AF wide-angle zoom lenses, then treat yourself. Although awesomely expensive, these high speed, versatile 20-35mm zooms, are really wonderful for landscapes and all manner of photography. The more cheaply priced Sigma 21-35mm f/3.5 - f/4.1, in the same genre, produces an excellent image, but is a bit darker to see through than the f/2.8 Canon/Nikon lenses.

Sigma 21-35mm

In the lightweight (most are about 270 g) wide-angle lens category of fixed focal length, the 24mm f/2.8 is a little gem. I suggest that you buy the one made by your camera manufacturer.

Next, a medium telephoto zoom. How about Sigma's recent 70 - 210mm f/4-f/5.6 APO AF lens? This lens is sharp and compact, has a handy zooming range and is reasonably priced. An APO or apochromatic lens is one which is highly corrected for three colours of the spectrum instead of the usual two. Put simply, an APO lens is a premium quality lens with an extremely crisp image with very high contrast.

Canon 80-200 f/2.8 zoom

The 80 - 200mm f/2.8 ED zooms (ED means that some elements in the lens design are made of high quality, low-dispersion glass), made by the leading camera makers and the independent lens manufacturers, generally have excellent optics for those in need of a brighter image and a faster lens in this zooming range. They are, however, considerably more expensive and heavier than the Sigma recommended above.

Canon 100mm macro

If you are interested in close-up photo-graphy try the macro/micro lenses in the 100mm to 105mm category made by the leading camera manufacturers. Check my suggestions in *Close-up Photography* in Chapter 7. One plea: if you want to do close-up photography use macro lenses rather than zoom lenses with close focusing facilities – zoom lenses are versatile but cannot do everything.

Big telephoto lenses

The new computer-designed AF telephoto lenses are easy to use and closer-focusing than the old manually focusing ones with conventional helical focusing. Many represent a major advance in optical quality, in that the calcium fluoride, or special low dispersion glass lens elements, keep red and blue light in better focus, resulting in excellent colour correction so that you get sharper, brighter pictures.

If you want to begin your photographic career with a strong interest in birds or other wildlife, then start saving for a suitable telephoto lens as soon as you can. The AF 300mm f/2.8 lens with a 2x tele-extender (see below) will produce a 600mm f/5.6, but you may decide to get a fast AF 600mm telephoto for photographing species such as wading birds which feed in flat open places where concealment for the photographer can be difficult. Under these conditions you will need a sturdy tripod and a photographic hide.

Tele-extenders

These are small auxiliary lenses composed of several elements which fit between a telephoto lens and the camera body. They increase the focal length of the master lens, either by doubling it, or increasing it by 1.4x. If, for example, you attach a 2x tele-extender to a 300mm lens it is converted into a 600mm lens. The 1.4x extender will alter the same lens to one with a focal length of 420mm.

There is a catch, however. The 2x tele-extender reduces the maximum aperture of any lens it is attached to by two f/stops, whereas the 1.4x reduces the maximum aperture by only one stop. This can be a bother in that it reduces the ability of your camera to focus quickly and accurately on to your subject. Most lenses slower than f/5.6 will hunt and will not autofocus properly in poor light.

Tele-extenders should be attached only to your best, fixed focal-length telephoto lenses and not to most zooms. These, in addition to multiplying the focal length by 1.4x or 2x, also multiply any residual aberrations of the prime lens by the same amount, so beware. The extender can only transmit the optical performance of the lens in front of it. Make sure the extender and the prime lens are made by the same company, otherwise off-centring of the photographed image and undesirable colour changes may occur.

One successful recipe is using a 2x extender with a 80 - 200mm f/2.8 ED lens: the result is a f/5.6 160 to 400mm lens. Used in this way extenders become handy devices to give your lenses more flexibility when you need it. My preference is for the 1.4x one, because you lose only one stop whilst still preserving a good quality image.

A comment about buying lenses

If you buy a new lens you should get to know it as soon as you can. Leave your other lenses behind and, for the first three weeks, take all your pictures with your new lens. Even if you want to photograph something with a wide-angle lens, and your new lens is a telephoto, get further back from your subject until your new telephoto lens gives you the coverage you want. In this way you'll gain a fresh insight into your subject, and at the same time get an image most people might not have thought of.

I would stress that beginners should start with the shorter focal-length lenses which are easy to handle and are forgiving when the inevitable mistakes are made. With them you can, in a gentle way, learn what lenses can and cannot do before you set out to buy the big and expensive telephoto lenses. Telephoto lenses have an extremely small depth-of-field, are prone to camera shake, and to image disturbance by reflected curtains of heat on a hot day. You will also need a large tripod capable of holding these longer focal length lenses absolutely rigid. In short, you need to have clearly in your mind what you want such lenses to do for you before committing your cheque book to one of them.

What is a good lens?

I'm often asked this. Essentially it is one that produces sharp images, has good contrast, and faithfully renders true colours – all with a minimum of image distortion. We can define a lens's sharpness as its ability both to produce fine detail (its resolving power) and ability to reproduce subtle differences in shade where they meet along a common border (its contrast). Poor contrast comes from light seepage into the dark areas on the film which will reduce the overall image sharpness. The ability of a lens to reproduce colours faithfully (its colour balance) probably causes a few grey hairs for the designers, and also for their computers. The lens manufacturer must take into account how the lens handles, how heavy it is, whether it is compact, durable, and of a practical design. And, of course, whether the customer can afford to buy it.

Lens tests

Lens tests show what a lens can do on a flat piece of paper with diminishingly small things written on it. Some people go grey worrying about the difference between 'very good' and 'excellent' or the 'Subjective Quality Factor' (SQF) of their lenses. Remember this: lenses are generally made for the purpose of photographing three dimensional subjects in the real world, such as landscapes, people, animals, buildings, flowers and the like. Hence anyone who tries to find out the truth solely on the basis of technical curves, or test charts, is likely to obtain a misleading impression of what a lens can do in real life.

You should be more interested in the actual photographic performance of a lens, rather than its reputed performance on paper. If I must check a lens, I prefer to shoot it through its f/stops at landscapes and the like, and then carefully compare the resulting images for conspicuous defects, such as resolution, contrast, vignetting, poor centring and colour balance. In this way I can quickly establish which are critically the best apertures to use with a particular lens, as well as unearthing any flaws the lens might have. I once found a very expensive Japanese lens which was poorly centred, so that the image was sharp on one side but not the other. I returned it to the wholesaler and got a new one. It's not a bad idea to run a test film through on any new lens you buy – and any second-hand one, too.

Buying used equipment

This requires care and some knowledge of cameras. Some hapless victims buy second-hand cameras that are true photographic bombs; shutters not working, lens mounts bent out of alignment: in short all sorts of problems associated with a device with hundreds of moving parts that is a camera. So beware.

I'll first discuss AF cameras, and then manually focusing cameras – just in case you're considering one of these.

Check any intended purchase carefully:

- Check the camera visually for any signs of external and internal damage by impact or sea corrosion.
- Are the battery contacts clean and uncorroded?
- Are the electronic lens terminals in the breech of the camera clean, secure, and undamaged?
- Is the on/off switch secure and not loose? Are there any sand grains or is dirt embedded around it or the shutter release button?
- Is the pressure plate clean and unscratched. Are all the film guide rollers clean and free-running? Is the foam padding around the film window still glued in securely and not warped?
- Is the flash shoe connection clean and secure?
- Is the display panel window clean and unscratched?
- Is the viewfinder clean and free of any debris?
- Are all screws there, and in new condition?

Check ALL electronic functions carefully. Does everything work? Check all the Programs, Shutter Priority, Aperture Priority, and Manual mode functions; check all the metering modes. Do delayed action blinkers blink? Does the flash fire properly? Does the camera autofocus properly (try lenses of varying focal lengths – and particularly large telephoto lenses if you can)? Does the camera load and rewind properly (check with a test film)? Is an electronic cable release there, and does it work? You cannot easily check the shutter visually because many AF camera shutters will not work properly with the back of the camera open, you will need to insert an old film and have a good ear. Make sure that you get an instruction book! And, most importantly, a fresh set of batteries.

AF lenses should be checked in the same way as manually focusing lenses (see below).

If you're not sure about doing all these checks yourself, get expert help. See if you can get some form of guarantee with your purchase. Once home, and before any guarantee expires, load a film in the camera and check all its operations promptly – examine the film for any faults – including any scratches which may herald pressure plate damage.

And now a check-list for manually operating cameras.

- Is there undue wear to the top and bottom plates or any small dents? Ask to see the camera case and instruction book.
- Is there any sign of tampering or repair? Are all the screws still there and in their original condition?
- Check to see whether the battery contacts are corroded or rusty.
- Are the shutter blinds or blades damaged, faded, or bent?
- Because the lens mount conveys a lot of information between a lens and the camera body, check carefully the mount's pins and levers for damage and undue wear.
- Is the film pressure-plate free of any scratches?
- Are the viewfinder and mirror completely clean of dirt and debris?
- Does the lightmeter work under extreme lighting conditions.

Testing the shutter

Checking the shutter is important. Set the shutter speed dial to one second and engage the delayed-action release. If the shutter is dry or faulty, the delayed action may creak into life only to stop before its full run. The shutter may open, and stay open.

The run of the slow gear-train should sound like one second and nothing faster, otherwise the faster shutter speeds may also be inaccurate. Modern quartz-timed shutters are accurate and usually stay accurate; it's the mechanical ones with small gears that can give trouble.

Next, remove the lens, open the back, and hold the camera up to a bright light. Fire it on its fastest speed– you should see a brief flash of light. Now select a slower shutter speed and watch for more light passing through. If you cannot see any light at high speeds the shutter is faulty, and the film will remain unexposed at these speeds. This fault can occur with all cameras, even very modern ones, so don't assume that a new-looking camera has a fail-proof shutter.

Finally, ask to have a small electronic flash fitted to the camera so that you can check whether the 'ready' light in the viewfinder lights up and the flash fires properly.

Checking lenses

When buying second-hand lenses, ensure that the diaphragm blades are clean and oil-free. If they aren't, the lens is useless without expensive repair. Put the lens on the camera and check whether it focuses correctly. Ensure that the elements within it are clean and secure. If the lens has a filter attached, check that it unscrews smoothly. If it doesn't, the lens has been dropped. Don't buy it.

Lens surfaces need to be clear and free of scratches and abrasions. A lens that has been cleaned with an abrasive cloth will be slightly dull because the lens coats have been damaged. Avoid such lenses.

All these simple tests will enable you to buy a camera worthy of taking pictures. When you buy any camera, have a new battery fitted, take a note of the serial numbers on the body and lenses, and have everything insured.

LENS HOODS

Lens hoods not only reduce unwanted light entering the lens, but also can help minimise damage to your lens if you inadvertently walk into a tree. It's better to put a dent in a lens hood than in your expensive lens.

Most telephoto lenses have a sliding lens hood built into them. Most macro lenses have a sufficiently large focusing mount to shield the front element of the lens from extraneous light and do not need a lens hood. Wide-angle lenses, however, because of their construction, do not usually have built-in lens hoods. Regardless of what sort of lens you are using, or whether you are shooting into or away from the sun, always fit a lens hood. It's simply a must.

Warning: Make sure that you buy the correct lens hood for the focal length of your lens: do not, for example, fit a 50mm lens hood on to your wide-angle lens. The result will be an image with dark, shadowy corners which we know as *vignetting*. This can also occur if you fit a lens hood over a filter and shoot with the lens stopped down to a small aperture.

FILTERS

There are a huge number of filters available to photographers. Most are gimmicky, razzle-dazzle things which you should ignore.

Four filters are useful for colour photography.

Skylight filters: these correct the bluish nature of some colour films or limit the amount of UV light entering the lens. Such filters are mostly used to protect lenses from salt spray, finger-marks and ice-cream. It is best to remove them for most photography, especially close-ups with flash, or where flare off their flat surfaces might ruin a good shot.

Polarising filters: these are invaluable for bright sunny days; polarising filters reduce reflections from non-metallic surfaces, heighten colour, and produce

dramatic skies. Excellent for landscapes. If your wide-angle lens takes a different sized filter to your other lenses, fit a polarising filter to it first, because you will probably want to start using such a filter for land scapes before trying its effects with other lenses. There are two types: circular for AF cameras that meter off the film plane and linear for all other types of cameras. If you have an autofocus camera, make sure that you get a circular polarising filter – otherwise the linear polarising filters will disrupt the ability of the camera to focus your lens properly.

Amber filters: on dull, overcast days, a bluish cast will frequently appear in colour transparencies. Amber filters, such as the 81A or A2, will correct this by compensating for the blueness. An invaluable filter for winter and heavily shaded subjects.

Soft-focus filters: these are special filters designed to produce a slight flare in your photographs. They are effective for portraiture and close-ups of flowers, and when you wish to create landscapes with an atmosphere created by a soft and flowing flare. There are two types: No. 1 which has mild effects and No. 2 which is stronger.

Notes:

1. Don't buy an expensive lens and put a cheap filter on it.

2. *Never screw more than one filter at one time on to a lens,* Dark, shadowy corners (vignetting) may appear on your transparencies, particularly with wide-angle lenses. You will also greatly increase the chance of un-wanted flare with two filters on your lens.

Slik 16 tripod.

TRIPODS

A good tripod is vital for successful nature photography. I cannot over-emphasize this. How sharp your image is depends mostly on the stability of your camera. Loss of sharpness is nearly always due to camera movement during exposure. A good tripod is as important as the film in your camera. Both are essential.

Nature photographers need a tripod that can collapse completely to the ground, such as the Slik 16 , the Velbon VEF 3 , or a Gitzo 224. These tripods have independently adjustable legs which allow you to set them up on uneven surfaces – important requirements for the nature photographer.

The 'pan and tilt' heads available for tripods are easier to handle than the small, ball and socket types. They also offer more support for your camera, particularly when using larger lenses. Make sure that the head has large, easy-to-use knobs that can readily be tightened and released. A quick-release shoe that comes away with the camera can be handy for photographers in a hurry. A device made by Slik, is a large, solid pistol grip, which makes altering your camera's position on your tripod exceptionally easy. I have one and can recommend it.

Some tripod manufacturers make tripod cases enabling you to carry your tripod more comfortably. You could either make one, or simply attach a carrying leather strap to your tripod.

If you must hand-hold your camera, use the focal length of your lens as a guide to minimum shutter speed (i.e. a 20mm lens can be hand-held at 1/20th of a second or faster, a 500mm lens at 1/500 of a second or faster, and so on). It is an old and useful rule of thumb. I generally avoid shooting anything slower than 1/30 of a second without using a tripod. Some people show off by announcing that they can hold their cameras rock steady at a quarter of a second. Just say, 'how interesting', and set up your tripod.

Cable releases and remote controllers

Most AF cameras now have convenient infra-red remotes that I've already mentioned. Other cameras have expensive electronic cable releases. The latter are, in my opinion, a big rip-off by the camera manufacturers. You can buy a relatively inexpensive adaptor that screws into your camera and allows a simple cable release to be fitted to it. Buy one and save money.

If your camera only takes the standard cable release, buy a relatively short one of about 30 cm in length. Many are black in colour and a dream to lose, so attach a piece of fluorescent orange tape to it. Mark your remote controller in a similar way if you want to keep it.

Batteries, and working in the cold

AF cameras devour batteries. Carry spare ones at all times. Lithium batteries last much longer than silver oxide or alkalines, but they're more expensive. Some batteries have a date stamped on their package which can be helpful in determining the date of manufacture.

Always remove batteries from electronic flashes and cameras if you don't plan on using them for several weeks. It's a good idea to write the date on a small tab inside the camera case when you put batteries into your camera. Use only long-life batteries. Replace any battery after one year's use, or sooner if you are working in cold climates. AF cameras working under cold conditions can last only about six to eight films before dying, so beware.

Some manufacturers provide an anti-cold battery pack which takes the place of the batteries in your camera. Anti-cold packs contain batteries in a small plastic container which is designed to slip into a warm pocket close to your body. Manual cameras with small gear trains inside them will freeze more readily than the printed circuits of AF cameras. The newer cameras are lubricated for life – providing they are not subjected to blowing sand or salt spray. An old or second-hand camera may need cleaning, but this can be expensive.

Camera bags

Select your camera bag with care. I use a Lowe Pro PhotoTrekker which I carry on my back. It has an adjustable interior to suit my changing needs. If you buy a bag to sling over your shoulder, make sure it has a waistband to secure it to your body, otherwise it can be clumsy, even dangerous, when you're descending a steep slope.

Tips on camera and lens care

Avoid lens tissues and lens cleaning liquids. An old, well-washed white cotton T-shirt or bedsheet, cut into handkerchief-sized pieces is better. Put them in a small, self-sealing plastic bag to keep them free from grit.

Lens brushes are useful. Try to find one with a brush that collapses into the rubber bulb and is sealed with a protective cap. And don't touch the brush hairs with your fingers because human skin is naturally oily. Pay paticular care NOT to touch the metal blinds of your camera's shutter.They are exceedingly thin and can deform easily if poked by a finger. And sometimes the tightly overlapping metal blinds will capture, and pull out, the hairs of lens brushes, leaving them to appear in the clear sky of your next slide.

To clean a lens, use your lens brush first to clean off any dust, then breathe lightly on the lens and wipe gently with your cloth. Use a separate cloth to clean the camera body. Do not use commercial air sprays.

To carry or store lenses conveniently, butt two lenses together. Do this by removing the rear lens caps and cementing them back to back using a *high strength* epoxy resin. The reason for the italics will become painfully obvious to those who ignore them.

To store your equipment, put it in plastic bags containing silica gel to absorb any moisture. If you have a mechanical camera make sure that the shutter of your camera is not tensioned, as this will put unnecessary strain on the shutter blind springs.

Having two camera bodies

If you can afford it, buy two camera bodies. The second body need not be new, so long as it is reliable and accepts the same lenses and accessories as your prime camera. Now you can put a fast film in one body, and a slow film in the other, while also having a spare if one of your camera bodies gets lost, or suffers from heart failure.

Insurance

Look after your camera equipment. Modern cameras can sometimes bounce quite neatly when they're dropped, but sometimes, too, they can shatter like an expensive egg. Keep them safe, and away from heat. Take a list of the serial numbers and insure your equipment under an 'all risks' policy with your insurance agent. If you go overseas, make certain that your insurance covers your equipment while you are out of the country. Keep your insurance up-to-date. See a customs agent before you take your camera equipment out of the country. Customs will 'sight' your equipment, record the serial numbers, and allow you to bring these items back into the country without incurring a glint in their eyes.

A warning

NEVER rely on your non-photographing friend to buy your new, cheap camera overseas for you. This is inviting a disaster. Not only will they be ripped off by sales sharks, but also the chances are high that they will return with the wrong gear for you.

Storing your slides

Because you have spent a lot of money on camera equipment, as well as time and effort in taking your pictures, it follows that you should take care of your slides when you get them returned from the processing laboratory. Beware of dust, fingermarks and scratches, and store slides in a cool dry place.

Slides can be stored in a number of ways:

- In the plastic containers they came in from the processing lab (handy, but not convenient for sorting them out)
- In a slide box or case which holds up to 700 slides (useful, but you have to take each slide out to view it).
- In clear plastic viewpacks which take 20-40 slides which either slide into small pockets or which sit snugly into recesses and have a stiff plastic sheet that clips over them, so that they cannot fall out. I use these myself. The plastic sheets are designed to hang on rails within a filing cabinet and each pack can be viewed easily, either by holding it up to a light, or by using a lightbox specially made for this purpose.
- Slides can also be stored in projector magazine trays. If you take a large number of slides this can prove convenient but it is rather expensive.

Dressing for the part

Be sensible. Wear warm clothing, particularly if you are taking close-ups of small flowers in cool windy places. Always have a windproof parka handy, as standing or crouching in one place for an hour can chill an unprotected body. Carrying a small piece of high-density foam to kneel on is a good idea, as is wearing waterproof footwear to avoid cold, wet feet. A good pair of lightweight boots are a must for most photographic forays into the field. Boots with worn soles can be dangerous to someone climbing or descending slopes with camera gear slung around their neck. Don't wear sneakers in wet, slippery places - they're positively dangerous. Wear a hat and mind your back, as crouching over something small for any length of time can damage your lower-back ligaments and your sense of well-being. When photographing animals, wear clothing that is inconspicuous.

MEDITATION
Fuji Velvia 50, Olympus mju 35-70 zoom. Hand held.
Pocket-sized point and shoot cameras can occasionally produce surreal images - even straight into the sun, where their lenses often flare very badly. But here, on this dreamy day, everything was at peace. The sun gleamed lazily on the sea, and the low swell breathed quietly on the rocks below. With this image I've tried to express that day on film.

LAKE SARAH

Fuji Velvia 50, Canon EOS 5 with Canon 28 - 80mm L zoom lens, f/11 at 1/15 sec. Tripod.
It's late autumn and the first mountain frosts have already arrived. The mist is quickly lifting from the lake, and strong side lighting illuminates part of the hillside, throwing it into bold relief, and casting reflections across the water. I used the small clump of rushes within the lake as a key element in this composition.

COLOUR AND TEXTURE
Fuji Velvia 50, Leica R5 with 100mm APO macro lens. 1/60 sec. at f/11. Tripod.
Strongly contrasting colour, rich texture, and repetitive lines all serve to make this image a fillip for the eye. Colour invigorates our vision: you should explore its potential to please.

There is no magic recipe for making good pictures. Every image maker marinates in their own ideas about composition. There are *no rules* for photographic composition, and don't let anyone convince you that there are. Some photographers spend their lives trapped by their own self-inflicted rules. Don't YOU be one of them.

What photographers try to do is to catch a moment in time, and make it timeless. It's your results that count, not how you achieved them. The underlying key to a good picture is your sensitivity to your subject, and your ability to create an atmosphere within the image.

Selecting a subject requires care. Ask yourself "Why do I like this scene? What is so eye-catching about it?" Try to isolate the special qualities of the scene that attract you. It may be the colours, or a specific colour, it may be a group of trees, or just one particular tree. Whatever it is, take the time to locate and consider it. Once you have identified your subject, the next step is what to include along with it.

Keys to good composition

A good image should impart the following:

Impact: it attracts and holds attention.

Simplicity: enables the viewer to find the subject easily.

Balance: balance is the linchpin to successful composition–balance between the units which make up the picture. Because each object in the composition has a definite attraction to the eye, each object will influence the others around it. All compete with each other for the attention of the viewer. Images can be organised on the basis of balance only, so that a visual anchor in the image is unnecessary.

Vitality: is there a sense of life in a picture? Action and movement can be obtained by the diagonal use of line and the diagonal use of contrast. When a diagonal line is alone or unsupported, it challenges our sense of gravity and conveys a sense of falling – hence the feeling of movement.

Unity: the image has a satisfying, coherent wholeness.

Mystery: gives the viewer's imagination something to ponder.

Time test: if you still like a photograph five years after you took it, the chances are that it was a good image.

THE VISCERAL TREE
Fuji Velvia 50. Photo by Di Forbes.
This image has an almost mystical quality about it. The twisting ribbons of roots, spreading downwards from the tree trunk, create an excellent foil for the balanced shapes of the adjacent rocks, while the predominating green throughout the softly lit image attracts and holds our attention. See if you, too, can find an unusual way to photograph the ordinary.

THE SENTINEL
Kodachrome 64, Olympus OM 1 with Zuiko 50-mm lens, f/5.6 at 1/60 sec.
Photo by Martin London.
This dark and brooding image is dominated by Martin's placement of the tree trunk in the centre of it. The pale sky in the background provides backlighting to the scene, and we can discern Black Swans resting on the lake's surface. Sombre weather, such as we see here, can produce powerful images.

Remember that great pictures are *made* not taken. And great pictures usually have a clearly defined *purpose* about them. You *know* what the photographer was trying to express.

Now let's reinforce the above guide-lines with a few practical ideas.

Putting it all together

The frame itself is a powerful tool in composing an image. Watch what you do with it and where you place it. Remember that *everything* within the viewfinder frame will appear on your film. So, first find your subject, then take great care what you include along with it. Avoid too much background, otherwise your subject may get lost in it. Give your subject the priority it deserves.

Which format? The *horizontal or landscape* format of 35mm cameras suggests stability, expanse, depth and restfulness, and encourages horizontal movement of the eye when viewing it. The *vertical* format suggests height and aspiration, and allows upward movement of the eye when viewing it.

Most images will benefit from a *visual anchor* to secure unity of interest, otherwise the eye will wander about without finding a point of rest. Many people fall into this trap when photographing landscapes: when we look at a picture of forest, with no visual anchor, we want to create one. We are dissatisfied.

Remember, too, that the eye tends to group things of similar size, shape and colour together whenever we read a photograph. Great compositional shapes to look for are rectangles and triangles and you will find a wealth of these everywhere in nature. Watch for interesting patterns, such as rows of windows on a building or ripples in a lake. If you have two areas of interest in your picture, look for ways of linking them together to form an interesting conclusion. The top of a picture can be appropriately linked to the bottom, by a waterfall for example, particularly if you capture the motion of the water by using a slow shutter speed. In the resulting picture the water looks like spun glass. Two people in a picture can be linked together by ensuring that they are looking either at each other, or at something inside or outside our field of view.

Not everything needs to be incorporated into the photograph. Viewers will fill in for themselves any aspects of your subject that are implied by the picture, but missing from it. We call this *closure*, and it can be effectively used to create interest and tension.

Other valuable aids are lines. The greatest horizontal line is, of course, the horizon. Horizontal lines are at peace with gravity; they denote calm and repose. Curving lines digress or meander peacefully. Vertical lines are full of protective strength and grandeur, like a strong tree trunk. Remember that a line is a very thin shape, and that lines can create shapes very easily. The difference between a line and an edge is subtle, but important lines will separate strongly contrasting colours like a razor, yet an edge – such as frost adhering to a leaf – will serve to outline the shape of the leaf and greatly enhance its shape.

Diagonal lines create movement and tension. The eye will follow strong diagonal lines wherever they lead. If they enter the picture, diagonal lines tend to create lines of perspective, such as an avenue of trees or a row of buildings down a street. Perspective is extremely useful in giving depth to an image. Perspective effects can also be induced by weather conditions. Haze or mist will soften and lighten a receding image which, in turn, gives an effective illusion of depth and space.

A sense of motion may be critically important to a photograph, depending on the subject. We can introduce motion by letting the subject do the moving for us, such as panning with a bird in flight or using a slow shutter speed to create movement in leaves rustling on a tree; or we can create the feeling of motion by directing the way in which the photograph is read.

Space before and behind the moving subject has a strong effect on the action. More space in front implies the subject is

THE LONG FORGOTTEN WINDOW
Fujichrome 50, Nikon FA with Nikkor 180mm lens, 1/15 sec. at f/11. Tripod. This weather-beaten window illustrates two points; the rule of thirds, and the interesting effect of putting a frame within a frame. Careful spot metering was required here to avoid my camera's lightmeter over-exposing the image because of the large black hole (upper left) leading to the house interior. I metered on the pale part of the window frame.

moving into the picture and not out of it. If large areas are left empty, or nearly so, this produces a suggestion of quiet and restfulness. If you require vigorous action, the picture space should be well- filled, with empty areas being avoided.

Find an interesting subject about as big as you are – something that you can walk around easily. Then load your camera with a 36-exposure film and explore your subject fully. Touch it, sit on it, get under it, in short, get to know its every aspect. Become it. The

SUNSET AND OYSTERCATCHERS
Fuji Velvia 50, Mamiya 645 Super, 105-210mm zoom lens, 2 secs at f/11. Tripod.
The sunset is quiet and peaceful, but the busy oystercatchers in the foreground add extra sizzle to this shot. I deliberately chose a slow shutter speed to blur the birds. A tripod and a slow shutter speed allow us fully to exploit the magic that our fleeting eyes miss.

first shots on your film will be easy, the last ones will not. Probably all your imagination will be required to complete the film. Ask to have your processed film returned unmounted, so that you can clearly see the differences between your first and last efforts. Big changes will occur between frames one and thirty-six. Write a memo to yourself in your head – "get closer, fill the frame".

Now try the opposite. Get very close to your subject – as close as your lens will allow. With each exposure, move back a bit. Instead of close-ups, you'll now discover shapes, lines, patterns, and space in your unfolding compositions. Exercises such as this will give you a valuable insight into how you perceive your environment, and will help improve your photographic awareness.

And, note too that most people tend to be more interested in the lower part of a photograph than on the upper half. It probably has to do with gravity, and the fact that objects in the lower half of a picture are generally closer to us. This is what most people expect – you may wish to be creatively different.

Tips for beginners

So much for ideas on what a good picture should be. If you are just starting out with a new camera, you might find the following exercises helpful.

LINDIS PASS IN WINTER
Fuji Velvia 50, Leica R5 with 180mm APO lens. 1/125 sec. at f/8. Tripod. Shapes and textures, plus a dab of passing sunlight provided the inspiration for this shot. Shooting from a tripod and carefully selecting the composition is the key to these images.

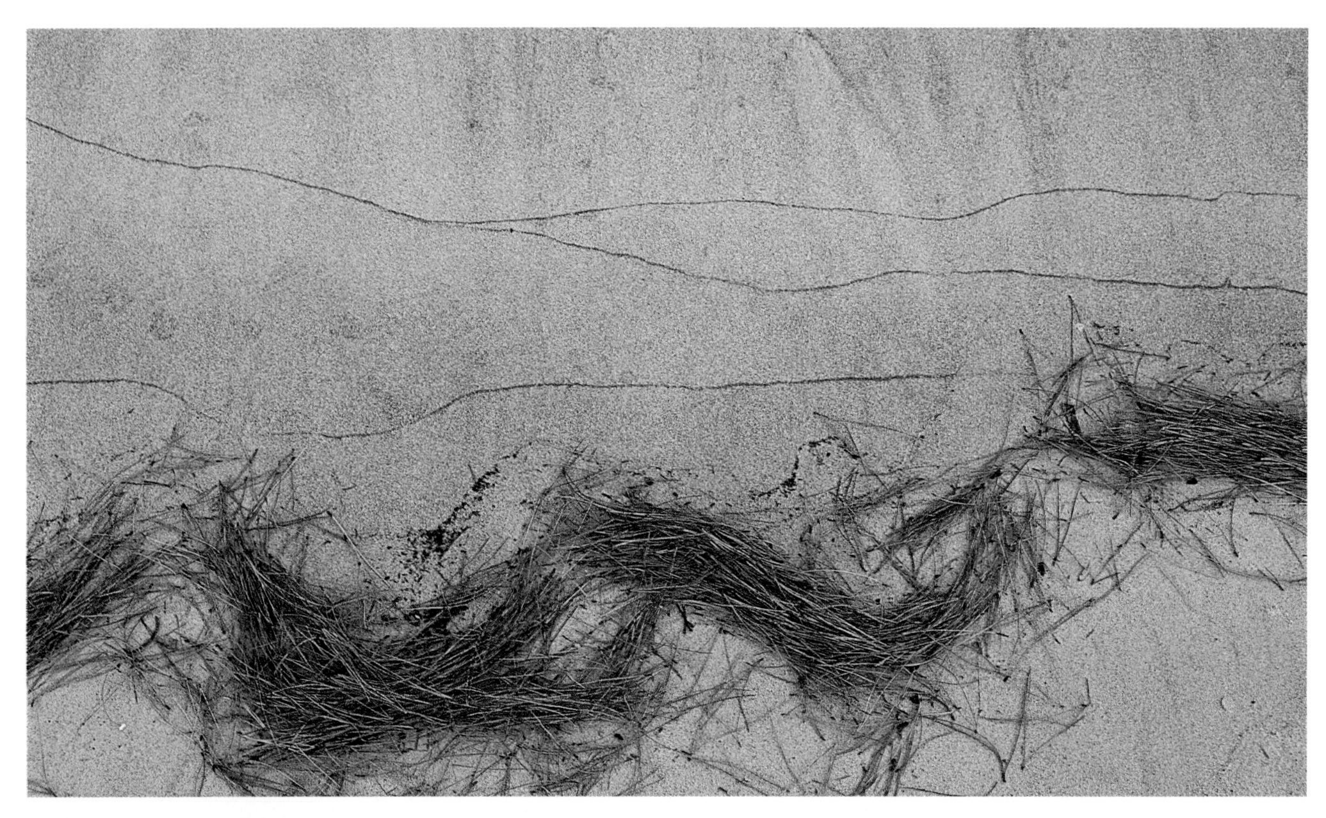

LANDSCAPE IN SAND
Fujichrome 50, Leica R5 with Leica 60mm macro lens, 1/30 sec. at f/5.6. Tripod.
A simple shot of a landscape created on fine sand by a gently lapping sea.
To see things creatively is the secret to good photography.

Also, be aware of the following

Avoid placing your subject dead centre in the frame unless you specifically want to emphasise symmetry. To place it slightly off centre will greatly improve the balance of the photograph. The old guide of dividing your frame into thirds and placing your subject on the intersection of these imaginary vertical or horizontal lines is a good way to begin.

Ask yourself whether your picture has a horizontal or vertical format. Try both before you commit yourself. Most beginners rarely get away from the horizontal format, so you need to make an effort to look for vertical images.

Prune out everything ambiguous, untidy, or boring that detracts from your chosen photographic subject. Climb over a fence rather than trying to include it; watch for power lines that will suddenly materialise from nowhere, and look out for unwelcome reflections. Watch too, that the sun isn't shining directly into your lens. Try to avoid things that are too close to the camera as they will be rendered out of focus in the final result.

Watch the light, remember that photographic films cannot accommodate too much light and too little light within a single exposure. Most beginners fall into this trap when photographing landscapes with a bright sky and a dark foreground. The result is a burnt out sky and a silhouette of nearly everything else. We can avoid this common mistake by limiting the amount of contrast in our images and photographing in light that is as even as possible everything within shadows, or everything in sunlight. Later, when you become familiar with your camera and your film, you will sometimes be able to exploit contrast to produce dramatic images.

Walk around your subject and carefully watch the changes in light. Do a lot of walking. Remember you are working with light, nothing else, so don't take a picture until you have positioned yourself to take advantage of the best light.

A word of caution – be careful not to disturb grass, sand, or snow that you might wish to use as a foreground. Most photographers will admit that somewhere during their careers they have ruined an excellent foreground by walking all over it in their search for the best camera position.

Avoid taking all your photographs from eye level like everyone else. Be different and alter your viewpoint. Get your knees wet, climb something – do anything to create novelty and interest in your pictures. Getting down to ground level is especially important for small plants, flowers, insects and the like.

And having the subject and its background together, well-balanced within your viewfinder, always scan the edges of your frame before you release the shutter. It's amazing to me how many people attempt to eliminate the intruding bits that impinge upon their framed image by simply pretending that they don't exist.

Once you get a feel for composition it can become fascinating in itself. As you master it, the thoughtful discipline which you used to begin with is replaced by the intuitive recognition of interweaving lines and balancing masses, and what finally feels right. Remember that your composition will gently fall somewhere along the leafy path between total order and complete chaos. Only you can determine its rightful resting place. Successful composition will bring a higher sense of beauty in your pictures and a happier appreciation from your audience.

And, let's not do away with spontaneity and invention! Compositional care is important, but sometimes we have to grab a picture – instantly, before it's gone. Intuitive shots like this can produce great images, but for most people getting their intuitive antennae 'quivering' requires a lot

AUTUMN TEXTURES
Fuji Velvia, Canon EOS 10 with Canon 80-200mm L zoom lens, f/11 at 1/15 sec. Tripod.
Two large triangles which make up this simple textural composition. Note how the differing shapes and colour of the leaves serve to complement each other, and how the black branches assist both in the composition and in heightening the contrast in this image.
The balance achieved here requires no other compositional ploy – such as a visual anchor.

ADELIE PENGUINS (Pygoscelis adeliae) ON SNOW BANK, TORGERSON ISLAND, ANTARCTIC PENINSULA.
Fuji Velvia 50, Olympus OM 4 with 65 - 200-mm Zuiko zoom lens.
Photo by Colin Monteath.
A beautifully composed shot, with a large grounded iceberg providing a very strong middle-distance focus, while the lively line of penguins streaming into the foreground create an attractive counterfoil to it.
The magical light and stunning landscapes of Antarctica provide the nature photographer with a feast of unforgetable visions.

THE LONE CABBAGE TREE
Kodak Gold 200.
Photo by Di Forbes.
The angled cylindrical shape of the tree trunk, with its dash of spiky green foliage, beautifully balances this composition into four large shapes. Balance is the key to a good photograph. Note, too, the pleasing tones and textures.

BLACK SWANS ON THE LAKE
Fujichrome 50 Professional, Mamiya 645 Super with 300-mm lens, f/8 at 1/8 sec. Tripod.
A telephoto lens allowed me to remove the extraneous matter to create this simple composition.The morning mist concealed all sense of a horizon, so adding a surreal air to this image. Mystery in a photograph adds greatly to its impact.

of practice and hard graft. An intuitive sense for a good photograph is ultimately far superior to any other way of capturing the ingredients which come together in a balanced photograph.

Telephoto lenses as a compositional aid

If you need to get closer, try a telephoto lens. Telephoto lenses tighten perspective, and enable you to be highly selective. If you have a busy subject full of many things, use your telephoto lens to scan it carefully. Several pictures may appear where, at first, you thought there was only one. Focusing is critical with telephoto lenses, and a good AF telephoto lens is certainly a boon to nature photographers.

Wide-angle lenses

Wide-angle lenses have the opposite effect to telephoto lenses. They push back the scene to create an effect of depth, space and airiness. They allow us to breathe. Such lenses are most useful for landscapes. Watch for an interesting foreground for your airy landscape that will provide perspective to your overall image. A slightly downwards angle will help create a feeling of depth in your image.

When you are hemmed in by the elements in your scene, and you want to create a bit of room in your image, a wide-angle lens is extremely handy. They also have the greatest apparent depth of field – I say 'apparent' because wide-angles don't really have more depth of field in an optical sense, it's just that they appear to have, because of their low magnification at a given camera-to-subject distance.

The wider the angle of view in a wide-angle lens, the more difficult they become to use. Composition becomes critical and distortion is conspicuous around the periphery of your image. The sun can now appear in your proposed image, generating

THE EARLY MORNING DIP
Fujichrome 50, Mamiya 645 Super with 300-mm lens, f/8 at 1/500 sec. Tripod.
Shot from 14 floors up in a hotel overlooking Queensland's Sunshine Coast, this image captures a strongly textured surf and its deep shadowing creates a lustrous rhythmic background for the young lady emerging from the water. Her positioning in the composition is important to its overall effect.

urge to take better ones? It's better to have one good picture than a hundred bad ones. After 28 years of photography I've only got about fifteen hundred slides to my name. Each of them is on probation until I get a better one.

Strive for sharpness of image, good composition and proper exposure. Has your image captured what you wanted to express? Did it achieve your purpose? Eventually you might come to terms with the most difficult lesson of photography – when NOT to press the shutter button.

Use a lightbox, a small slide viewer, or a projector to analyse your work. Seek criticism if that is what you want; but try to avoid photographic competitions, at least until your work is up to a suitable standard. I find it rather odd that a slide, which one judge dismisses, can win honours from another. Photographic competitions are often rather pompous, crushing affairs. Some people end up taking photographs not for themselves, but to cater to the whim of a judge. Be sensible. You be the critical judge of your own work. Craft your own style according to what *you* like.

What is a good photographer?

So much for what a good photograph might be. Who is responsible for it? Who or what is a good photographer?

The good photographer must have a keen desire to portray something. A picture should clearly express what the image-maker felt and thought about the subject at the time. This isn't necessarily the same reaction as that which will be experienced by the observer who views your picture. Because a photograph reflects the personality

REFLECTIONS ON A JERSEY
Fujichrome 50, Nikon FM2 with Tokina 90mm macro lens, f/22 at several seconds exposure. Tripod. Photo by Lynn Hutton.
A brightly patterned jersey, lying on a footpath, and photographed from inside through a window pane covered in dew, gave rise to this intriguing image. Creativity is what photography is all about.

MAINE FALL
Fujichrome 100. Olympus OM 1 with Zuiko 35-70mm zoom lens, f/22 at 1/4 sec. Tripod. Photo by Martin London. Here the strong vertical elements created by the dark tree trunks set up a well balanced composition, and when this is offset with the brilliant colour of the autumnal leaves we have an attractive and successful shot. When attempting such images yourselves, always ensure that the balance in your photograph is right, then your image will be a successful one.

of the photographer – how he or she perceives their environment – an observer can gain valuable insights into the photographer's psyche. In a sense, there is a contract between the photographer and the observer. The image-maker puts time and thought into creating an image; it is then necessary for the observer to spend time and thought in carefully evaluating the result. If the experiment works, both sides are enriched, and should rightly consider their time and effort well spent.

Good photographers never stop experimenting and learning from what they're doing. They're thinking: "Need this picture be correctly exposed? Need it be perfectly in focus? Suppose I over-exposed this, or placed it out of focus. What would happen? I'll try and see!" They spend time learning the so-called 'rules' of photography, and then break them, regularly. Compositional guidelines are only signposts to help you find your own vision, your own style. Don't tether yourself to them.

Practical ways to be a good photographer

Good photographers know their equipment well. Their cameras may look as if they've been used as a rock from a bird roost, but good photographers can grab anything in their camera bags without pausing to think about how it works. They know intuitively what it will do when they're faced with a picture-making opportunity.

A good photographer usually plans things in advance. What cameras and lenses will I need today? When should I be there? Where should I position myself before the event occurs? If they haven't been to the location before and it's reasonably handy, they'll check it out, note the light and find the best vantage point.

Good photographers always check their AF cameras before they return them to their camera bags. Camera switched off? Exposure compensation returned to zero? ISO rating what it should be? Lens returned to its infinity setting so that it will fit easily back into its case or compartment? Lens caps on? Filters all there and in the right place? And finally, where's the remote cable release? These spot checks can be done in a few seconds, and will save precious time (and money) next time you need your camera.

Good photographers keep their camera bags free of rubbish and keep their fresh film well separated from exposed film. Ask someone who has reloaded an exposed film back into their camera! Cameras that rewind films all the way back into the cassette can be very helpful in avoiding this.

A good photographer keeps a photographic diary wherein everything is written down. Where, when, what, how, why: good things, bad things. Feelings and experiences while collecting photographs. In short, everything that might help make a better shot next time.

Good photographers always carry far more film than they think they'll need on the day. Because they know that film is the cheapest item in their bag. Nothing is worse than running out of film.

Finally

Try to plan and evaluate any image that you are about to make. Experienced photographers may take four days to plan a picture, four hours to set up their optimum approach and only one second to take it. Pushing the shutter release is the easiest part of committing vision to film.

Always challenge yourself to do better and try not to imitate others. If you want to be a pictorialist and concentrate on pretty pictures, fine, be one. Just be the best you can at it.

Try not to get in a rut with your pictures. Set a blowtorch to your ideas occasionally. Stop and imagine what, if it is a living creature, your subject might be thinking of YOU, rather than what you're thinking about your subject.

Finally, and most importantly, remember this: without joy in your photography you have nothing. You will never put your best creative efforts into something you do not enjoy.

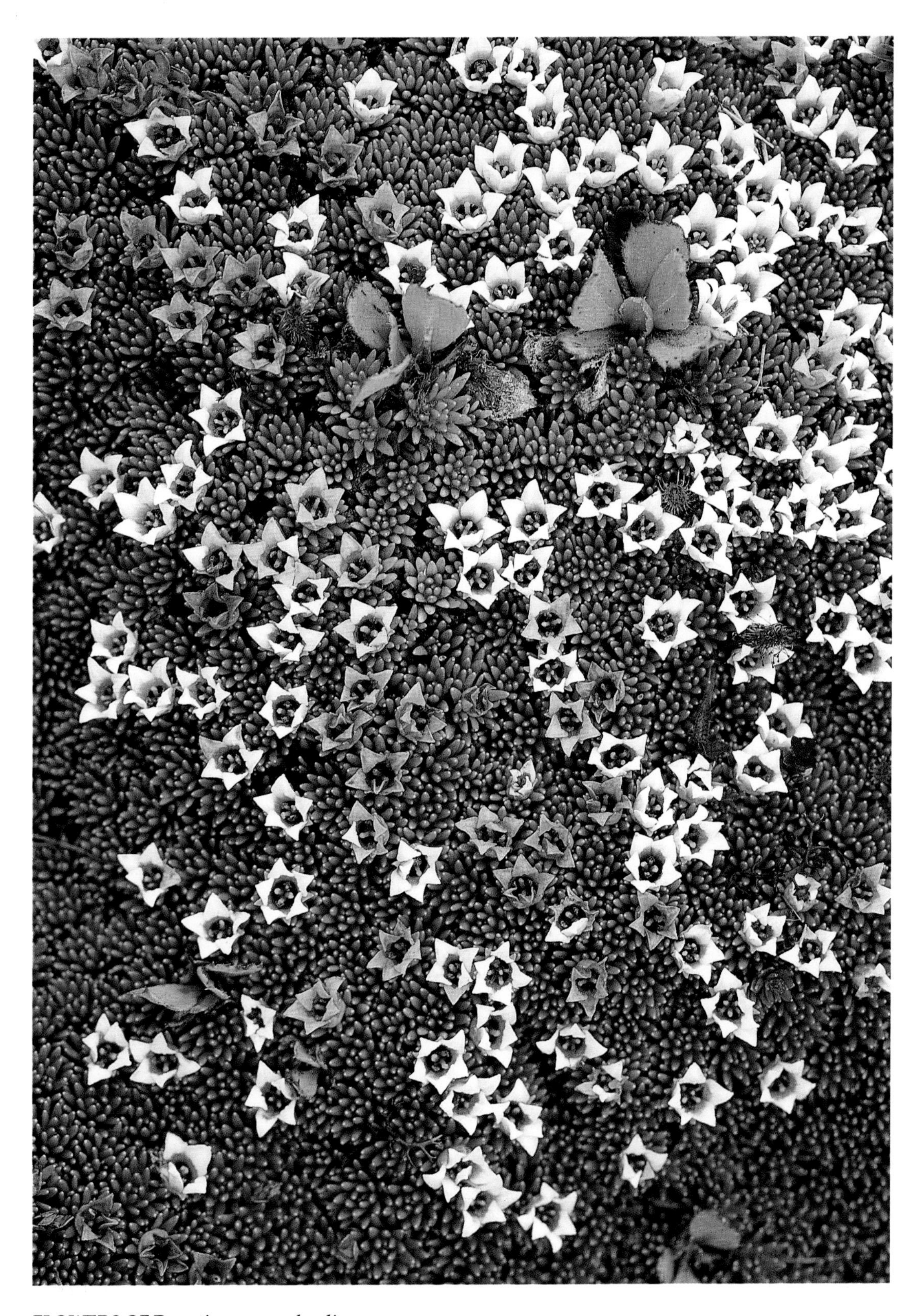

FLOWERS OF Donatia novae-zelandiae

Fujichrome Velvia 50, Mamiya 645 Super with 80mm macro lens, f/11 at 1/8 sec. Tripod.
Mother Nature creates the greatest compositions for us to find. This image is of an alpine ground-hugging cushion plant, so named because of its densely packed fleshy leaves, amongst which many small white flowers appear in summer. Selecting a composition here requires careful attention to the good use of available space in the frame of your viewfinder. A foam pad to kneel on will save you from wet, stiff knees, when you are trying to capture close-ups in damp peaty places around alpine tarns.

ELECTRIC STORM

Kodacolor Gold 100, Olympus OM1 with Zuiko 35-70mm zoom lens, shutter on Bulb. Tripod. Photo by Martin London.
Luck and instinct plays an important role in photographing lightning flashes. It's a matter of opening the shutter and pointing the camera in the right direction and crossing your fingers. Wide-angle lenses can help in getting more flashes on film, but be careful as the lightning flashes may appear too small in the final image. When they light up the brooding clouds, as shown in Martin's shot, so much the better.

EARLY MORNING ON MOUNT RUAPEHU
Fujichrome 50 Professional, Nikon F4 with Nikkor 105mm macro lens, f/16 at 1/2 sec. Tripod.
The low sun created this strongly textural shot. Note how the rim lighting of the foreground lava edges and the clump of back-lit tussock create an attractive fulcrum for the brightly-lit middle ground. The mosses provide a dab of colour to the scene.

Light is photography. Landscape photographers certainly worry about the light more than anything else. They gaze at the sky and squint a lot, because they know light is worth watching very closely. It controls how their images will appear on film. Good photographers actively explore light in all its nuances; they delight in responding to its colour and form – they marvel at how it creates shapes, texture, lines and perspective. It's a good thing night intervenes so regularly, otherwise many of them would never come home to roost.

Light is either *direct* or *soft*. Bright sunlight creates a brilliant directional light that creates strong contrast between where it falls and where it does not.

Directional light can be variable, it can come from the:

Front: light falls on the part of the subject nearest to the camera and shadows are small.

Side: light approaches the subject from the side, creating long shadows that fall across it, and thus creates strong texture and contrast.

Back: here the camera is facing the light source, so that the portion of the subject facing the camera is silhouetted and usually in deep shadow (backlit).

Soft or suffused light is one of the nature photographer's best friends. It occurs whenever sunlight is blocked and the light rays are scattered - clouds do this beautifully, and so do forest trees. Watch the way the light changes in the forest when the direct

BACKLIGHTING
Fujichrome 50, Nikon FA with Tokina 90mm macro lens, f/16 at 1/30 sec. Tripod. Photo by Paul Kennedy.
A good example of backlighting, here on ***Echium vulgaris****. The strong light is coming from a low angle in front of the camera. Note the repetitive triangles created by the bright flowers against the dark shadows behind them. Note, too, the brightly lit edge to the leaves which accentuates their shape.*

KEEP IT SIMPLE
Fujichrome 50 Professional, Leica R5 with 180mm APO lens, 1/4 sec. at f/11. Tripod. I used centre-weighted metering for this early morning shot of mist rising from a mountain lake. Rim lighting often creates a beautiful edge to a shape. The well-expressed simple shots make the best images.

QUIET LIGHT
Fuji Velvia 50, Ricoh KR10 with Tamron 70-210mm lens. f/16, shutter speed not recorded. Photo by Jane Macleod. The bright light on the sunken fence contrasts beautifully with the muted tones of the quiet background. Note the use of rectangles and triangles in this unusual but effective composition.

CASTLE COMBE
Ektachrome 100. Olympus OM 4 with Zuiko 24mm wide-angle lens. Exposure details not recorded.
Photo by Matheson Beaumont.
An excellent example of side-lighting caressing a peaceful English scene. Note how the light illuminates the texture and triangular shapes of the house structures, and the rough grassy roadway in front of them; note, too, how the bright chimney smoke helps enlighten the scene, and softens the strong lines of perspective. Matheson used spot-metering for this shot. Always be on the alert for the wonderful beauty crafted by side-lighting.

sun, with its strong slanting light burning bright pools of light on the forest floor, is obscured by a passing cloud. The light abruptly loses its intensity and contrast, and the forest details spring to life. Shadows, once strong and bold, are now soft and muted.

Light is greatly influenced by four factors: season, weather, time of day and distance from the equator. Early morning and late afternoon light is the best time of day for most photographers, and spring, winter, and autumn are mostly good times of the year. Summer is the best for alpine flowers and for taking close-ups of nature. Photographers working during the summer months in high latitudes have the special magic of continuous low-angled sunlight to enjoy. The day's dawns and dusks are greatly elongated in the Arctic and Antarctic.

The sun's march

Before sunrise, the air is still and the colours delicate and quiet. The landscape still slumbers. A great time for quiet light and great photography.

With sunrise comes rebirth and transformation. The land, the sea and the sky now lie awash in the sun's glorious and dramatic glow, with long, slanting shadows and brilliant contrast. The early morning light changes rapidly, so pay particular care to your exposure times: expect them to change very rapidly. You must be quick to capture these magic moments before they are gone, swept away, by the sun's march into the sky.

By noon the sun hangs high overhead, creating a flat and unrelenting light. Images made now have low contrast and fine clarity

SEA CLIFF TEXTURES

Fuji Velvia 50, Canon EOS 5 with Canon 28 - 80mm L zoom lens at 28mm, f/16 at 1/15 and 1/4 sec. Tripod.

Two images exploiting a marvellously eroded seacliff. In the first image, the angle of the bright autumnal sunlight meant that the entire face of the seacliff was cast in shadow, but enough reflected light was being thrown back towards the cliff from the nearby surf. Thus, provided with plenty of soft shadowless light, I was able to explore the varying planes of textures and tones in the cliff. The warm light created by a setting autumnal sun helped create the second shot on a return visit several weeks later. Note the complete change in emphasis.

DESERT MORNING
Fujichrome 100, Olympus OM 4Ti with 24mm wide-angle lens, f/5.6 at 1/125 sec. Hand held. Photo by Bevan Tulett.
The warm low light skimming across the sand has created a wonderful atmosphere for this desert landscape. The attractively lit camel, with its handsome passenger, adds a vibrant anchor to the composition.

of detail. This is the time for the pure colours that your film has been calibrated to record best.

Afternoons provide the warm, drowsy light we know so well. Strong side-lighting again returns to greatly enhance and mould the landscape, accentuating form and giving it a sense of depth and substance. The photographer walks, stops, ponders, and explores, marvelling at the tapestry of colour and light. As the sun sinks lower, the landscape fades with haze, and shadows sprawl beneath the sinking sun. Travel photographers revel in this time of day. Only the sunset remains before nightfall.

Shooting with, and against the sun

Shooting with the sun creates pictures of low contrast and good detail. Side-lighting creates strong contrast and shadow. Backlighting is a form of strongly directional light that tends to simplify our images by deleting detail to produce silhouettes. With backlighting try overexposing your pictures by a stop or two to create in them a mood of mellowness.

Shooting into the sun requires care. Lens hoods can help, but flare is a constant danger. Against the sun, zoom lenses and filters generate unwanted rainbows of colour, so try to avoid both of these. Use a lens of fixed focal length, no filters, and shade your lens if possible. Shooting from under a tree or other object with some protective shadowing helps greatly.

The 'sunny f/16 rule'

If you are out in bright sunshine and your camera's lightmeter fails, remember the 'sunny f/16 rule'. It's been a favourite for many photographers over the years.

Put your lens aperture on f/16 and use the closest shutter speed equivalent to the speed of your film. If, for example, you are using Fuji Velvia 50 ISO, select 1/60; if Fujichrome 100, use 1/125 of a second. The sunny f/16 rule works well provided that bright sunshine is available. Once you have set your calibration at f/16 you can, of course, change this to suit you needs. f/16 at 1/60 is essentially the same as f/ 11 at 1/125 or f/8

PAINTING WITH LIGHT
Fujichrome 50 Professional, Mamiya 645 Super with 300mm telephoto lens. f/5.6 1/2 sec. Tripod.
Nepal's sacred mountain, the 22,900 foot Macchapucchare. The mountain is about 30 miles distant from my camera location in the township of Pokhara. Notice the birds in the tree – deliberately out of focus, but adding their bit to the air of excitement of a new day dawning. Watching the sunrise creep down the mountains of the Himalaya for the first time was, for me, a breathtaking and spiritual experience.

A STORM APPROACHING A SMALL ICEBERG IN PARADISE BAY, ANTARCTIC PENINSULA.
Fuji Velvia 50, Olympus OM 4 with Zuiko 24mm lens. Photo by Colin Monteath. Strong sunlight has transformed this iceberg into a subject vibrant with texture and subtle colouring. The brooding sky has been tightly cropped to create a strong contrast to the gleaming ice. A great image has resulted from the photographer's vision.

at 1/250 or f/5.6 at 1/500 and so on. The faster the shutter speed, the larger the aperture; the slower the speed, the smaller the aperture. This relationship will soon become familiar to you. When experimenting, compare the readings your camera suggests with the settings presented by the sunny f/16 rule. Take notes in your logbook and if your camera needs adjusting, either alter the film speed or use the exposure compensation dial. It is a good habit periodically to check your lightmeter in this way.

The dangers of too much contrast

The direction and intensity of light is especially important to those of us who use colour transparency film. Colour film cannot cope with too much contrast – the difference in the light intensity between the bright areas in the photograph and the deep shadows that might also be present. Watch out for this. Too much contrast results in more images disappearing into waste baskets than for any other reason – at least now that autofocusing prevents fuzzy images being a valid excuse.

On a bright day with plenty of sunshine and shadows, watch how you frame a shot. Avoid bright skies and dark foregrounds by selecting one or the other – not both. Avoid bright reflections that might plunge the rest of your image into complete darkness or silhouette. Be on the look out for ways to reduce contrast – even waiting for a cloud to cover the sun briefly can be helpful in securing an image that otherwise might have had too much contrast.

Changing weather

Bright sun is useful for a few subjects, but certainly not for everything. When clouds block strong sunlight, a gentle light with soft shadowing can be produced. Since the contrast is low, the limited latitude of colour film can maintain all the detail within a

scene, and this can produce great pictures – where the quality of your lens, and the resolution and contrast of your film, can provide the best opportunities for you to produce a successful image full of detail and nuances of tone.

Muted light is especially good for forest interiors and close-up photography. However, because high overcast cloud naturally reduces the amount of available light, exposure times will be slower than bright sunlight, so your tripod will be necessary under these conditions. Watch carefully for any gusts of wind disrupting your long exposures.

Bad weather

Bad weather is good weather for photographers. It creates wonderful opportunities to photograph dark images with plenty of atmosphere.

If you are on the coast photographing a violent sea driven by a wailing wind, leave the protective skylight filter on your lens because salt spray can severely damage delicate lens coatings. Make sure you clean your equipment thoroughly as soon as you can. Wash your cleaning cloth to prevent salt on it smearing any clean lens surface.

AFTERNOON LIGHT ON THE LAKE
Fujichrome 50 Professional, Nikon FA with Tokina 28-70mm ATX zoom. f/8 at 1/4 sec. Tripod.
This image was created using a combination of muted sidelighting and a lack of wind, inducing reflections in the lake's surface. The overall effect is one of ethereal tranquillity. The quiet near sunset is always a special time for nature photographers.

LAKE SARAH
Fuji Velvia 50, Canon EOS 5 with Canon 100-300mm L zoom lens, f/11 at 1/30 sec. Tripod.
Another composition of Lake Sarah, this time using a longer lens. Here I have zoomed closer, and deliberately underexposed the image by one stop in order to accentuate the atmosphere. The clump of rushes is still retained in the composition, but the emphasis in the image is now much changed from my earlier one.
Try to explore your interesting landscapes by using differing lenses, and by altering your camera's exposure times. Remember to change your shutter speeds, not your f/stops, otherwise you could unduly limit the depth-of-field in your image.

SUNDOWN AT SOUTH BAY
Fujichrome 100 rated at 250, Nikon F4 with Nikkor 80-200mm zoom lens, f/11 at 1/250 sec. Hand held. Photo by Paul Kennedy.
Paul regularly passes this beach in the course of his work. If surf and sun are right, a photograph results. Motto is: if you find a photogenic place that you can regularly visit, always stop and check it out. Attend to its moods. Your patience will be rewarded with images that capture the soul of a place.

In rain or drizzle avoid getting your camera wet, this can be done by shooting from a car or hide, or by using an umbrella. Even though most circuit boards in AF cameras are specially treated to repel moisture, AF cameras don't like getting wet. During very wet weather put your camera in a plastic bag with holes in it for the lens and viewfinder. Watch out for condensation on your camera. If you're setting off to a district known for its rain and mist, where the humidity is high, place all your equipment in plastic bags containing sachets of silica-gel. It's a pain getting your gear in and out of plastic bags, but if you protect your camera it will remain reliable for years. Once back from your outing, remove camera equipment from their bags, and place the silica-gel somewhere warm where it can recover and fully dry out. A hair dryer – on LOW heat and LOW speed can help dry your gear as well as your hair. It is important that after a wet day working in the field you remove the batteries from your autofocus camera and carefully wipe them with a dry cloth. This will prevent the camera flashing signals at you the following day, indicating that it's not feeling well.

WINTER'S DELIGHT

Fuji Velvia 50, Leica R5 with Leitz APO Telyt 180mm telephoto lens., f/16 at 4 sec. Tripod.
Severe winter frosts can create wonderful images in the mountains. Here a beech tree has succumbed to the elements and now lies on its side, lost, but not forgotten. The hoar frost has adorned its limbs and the stream bed below in a wonderful panoply of white. In such scenes there is often a lot of blue light about, which can darken a photographic image and greatly alter the colour balance. You can compensate for this by using an amber warming filter and overexposing the image by about one to 1.5 stops. The blue colour bias can, however, create a cold atmosphere to your image, which you might decide is appropriate under the circumstances!

Photography is a compelling visual language, and nowhere can this be more beautifully expressed than in the rhythm of a landscape. But capturing a landscape isn't easy. They're not as simple to capture as they look. The landscape always leads in its dance with the photographer. It is we who must do the searching, the contemplating, the watching and the waiting. It is we who must express our image from the available light, or wait until the light is right.

Do you want to collect attractive landscapes, or to show the land the way it really is – sometimes bleak, dim, and forbidding? Grey skies and looming landscapes can generate powerful pictures which appeal to our sense of drama rather than the idealized scenes of landscape we see on picture postcards. The photographer of landscapes would do well to consider these points of view, but it all comes back in the end to what you want to portray and why. And remember, if an image fails to reflect our motivation of why we wanted to take the picture in the first place it will surely end up in the rubbish bin.

Landscape photography requires a good understanding of light: it often requires planning, practice, patience and good humour. Above all, it requires an abiding love for the land. If you're prepared to put in the effort, the landscape will delight and challenge you until either you cease to breathe, or drop your camera down a cliff.

Landscapes require us to be flexible in our approach to them. Be spontaneous – if the light is right. Plan meticulously – if need be. Careful planning will allow you to be spontaneous on the day. If you're not prepared to go with the flow, then landscape photography will be difficult for you.

Although landscapes remain where they are, much happens to them. They live in constant transformation from sunrise to sundown. The quality of the light, and the angle at which the light strikes the land can

THE SUN RETURNS
Kodachrome 64, Olympus OM 1, with Zuiko 50mm lens, f/16 at 1/15 sec. Tripod. Photo by Martin London.
Using strong side-lighting and a reflective surface, Martin has crafted a wonderful image here. Note the beautiful intersection of shadows and reflections in the water, and the high key-light amongst the branches of the trees. Such beauty expressed on film is the art and joy of the nature photographer.

THE MAGIC FOREST
Fuji Velvia 50, Leica R5 with 24mm lens, 1 sec. at f/16. Tripod.
Note the faerie-like quality of the subdued light here. It's created by an overcast day and a complete lack of wind. Try to avoid taking forest interiors in bright sunlight – our eyes can cope with the bright pools of light and deep shadows, but such subjects have far too much contrast for colour film to handle.

totally remodel its character in moments. The seasons, too, craft the colours of a landscape so completely that, from midsummer to midwinter, the same piece of country can become barely recognisable to the careless observer. Spring greens dry to summer browns, then autumn crimsons and yellows give way to the dark bare limbs of winter. The human element in the countryside is strong and vibrant, too: the farmer's toil can convert a tilled brown hill-side into a brilliant yellow when the rape plants flower. In these ever-changing passages of time lie constant delights for the landscape photographer.

You should try varying your viewpoints and bracketing your exposures by first taking a picture the way your lightmeter suggests, then using the exposure compensation control to over-expose by about two-thirds of a stop (+0.7) and underexpose by the same amount (-0.7). When you come to examine the developed film, check your bracketed exposures carefully. Notice how the slight change in exposure alters the mood of the picture. Which do you like most, and why? Remember that your lightmeter is a friend only, not your master.

If you consistently find that you prefer the slightly underexposed images you might decide to compensate for this by increasing the nominal ISO rating of that particular film. I find my camera gives better pictures on Fuji Velvia film when this film is rated at 50 ISO in bright light; in dull lighting I set my camera for the same film as if its rating was 40 ISO.

If you don't see a landscape ready for your camera, keep looking, appraise each bit of country as you round every corner in the road. I find myself frequently backing my car up, sighting down valleys comparing the viewpoints of different lenses in my mind's eye, and asking myself whether the scene will look better in the afternoon when I return home. I'll often stop and take a couple of pictures then, just in case. I do a lot of walking, too. Many wonderful landscapes lie far from any road. In the forest, look all around you. The trees overhead can form wonderful tapestries against the sky, and the sunlight filtering through the trees can create images of great beauty. Morning mists on a lake can do likewise. Remember that from moment to moment each scene is unique – it will never be exactly the same again.

try different lenses on your landscape. Don't expect to use only wide-angled lenses with sweeping vistas. Medium telephoto lenses can produce powerful landscape images too.

Foregrounds

In landscape photography foregrounds are extremely important. You can create a fine feeling of distance with a carefully crafted foreground. Overhanging branches can, for example, be used effectively in two ways – to soften the stark effect of the picture's frame, and to cut the contrast between a bright sky and dark land by allowing the trees leaves to drape across the sky in a natural curtain. Such framing material should relate to the subject of your photograph in some way, so that the image is integrated into a coherant whole.

FACE OF THE GLACIER
Fuji Velvia 50, Canon EOS 5 with Canon 100-300mm L zoom lens, f/11 at 1/2 sec. Tripod.
Franz Josef Glacier, in New Zealand, is currently grinding and crunching away, at about one metre per day, from its source in the mountains above into the lower bush-clad valley. This painterly image captures some of the interesting shapes and textures on the glacier's surface near its snout.

Landscape photography mostly requires the use of a good tripod. Ensure that your image is sharp by checking it carefully with the camera's depth-of-field preview button, and check that the horizon is straight before committing it to film. These things are much easier to check if the camera is on a tripod rather than hand-held. And don't forget to

Sometimes you can effectively drop the foreground out of your picture completely, to create a surreal image of landscape that looks as though it's hanging suspended in space. Whatever you do with foregrounds, don't ignore them.

The sky

Landscapes often involve the sky and you need to consider the sky with care. How dominant will it be in your photograph? If the sky is drab and uninteresting, then the photograph must necessarily dwell on the land itself, with the sky reduced as much as possible. Alternatively, there are times of the day and season, particularly in late summer, when enormous cumulo-nimbus clouds tower like cathedrals in the sky, forming magnificent skyscapes which completely overshadow and dominate the land below. Remember that the sky can be just as evocative and just as exciting as the land or sea. It is the skilful integration of an interesting sky with the patchwork of land that is a never-ending challenge to the photographer. Don't forget that a polarising filter can do dramatic things with skies, so try one if you think your image might benefit from it.

Coasts

There are few more absorbing places to find pictures than where land meets sea. Here can be found a great variety of scenery, a magnificent range of moods, and many examples of nature's sculpturing amongst the hard and soft rocks along the shoreline. A quiet sea brings a deep feeling of peaceful contemplation to most of us, and walking along a coast with a camera in this reflective mood can help us generate very expressive images. Many times have I walked along beaches in raging storms, and marvelled at the fury and power of the wind and sea.

Wide-angle lenses are particularly useful in capturing all the drama of the sea coast, as well as the sweeping vistas of land, sea, and sky. Fast shutter speeds will stop both huge curling waves and the delicate patterns of spent wave eddies drifting along the beach. Try deliberately underexposing your pictures to add zest and detail. About half a stop will do.

Next, try a different lens, perhaps a 180mm or 200mm telephoto, to explore the sea or coastline for that hidden picture. Watch the light, particularly if clouds are about, because the sun shining across rolling surf adds a warmth which can vanish if it is momentarily hidden by clouds.

WINDOW ON A DESERT LANDSCAPE

Fuji Velvia 50, Pentax 645 with 80 - 160mm zoom lens. Photo by Alan Pond. This fine desert shot, powerfully framed in rock, forces our eye through the created frame to the blue skies and open spaces of the Arizona's Monument Valley beyond. Deserts can be flat unrelenting places – the creative use of a natural frame will add great strength to the resulting image.

Pay particular attention to the effects of the polarising filter when using a wide-angle lens. The wider the angle of view, the greater is the variation in polarising effect that will appear from one side of the picture to the other. Polarising filters work best when 90 degrees from the sun, so that a lens covering 84 degrees will produce a slide with little polarisation near the sun, to full polarisation 90 degrees from it. The greatest effect will probably appear in the sky, where it will appear light blue near the sun, and very dark blue at right angles to it.

A polarising filter used at a non-polarising angle to the sun essentially acts as a neutral-density filter with a light reduction of about two and a half f/stops.

Water

The patchwork of colour in waterscapes is quite different to that on the land, and each affects our emotions in different ways. Both the sight and sound of water tends to relax us. Even the nodding reflections off water beamed on to a wall can have a soporific effect, water making us want to curl up and snooze.

Lakes contain and subdue water in a quiet, restful, way. When photographing lakes, you will often need a foreground to provide compositional support for your picture. The foreground might be a clump of rushes or trees at the lake edge, a wharf jutting out into the water or a fisherman standing heron-like in his thigh-waders. If the weather is fine and tranquil, the stones beneath the water along the shoreline can provide an interesting introduction to a lake stretching away to the horizon. Gleaming sunlight tracing a fiery path across the surface can add a most attractive highlight to any body of water.

Reflections provide symmetry of shape and colour, and allow us to break the 'rule of thirds' to place the horizon on or near the centre of the photograph. Anything reflected in water takes on a new stature – be it a

COASTAL SCENE
Fuji Velvia 50, Leica R5 with 35mm lens 1/250 sec. at f/5.6. Hand held.
It is the wonderful light in this landscape that brings it to life. I used a polarising filter to strengthen the mountain detail in the distance. And yes, I did wait for the three gulls to all face the same way. Note how they bring an element of tension to the scene – a sense of impending escape.

FOREST WATERFALL
Fuji Velvia 50, Canon EOS 10 with Tokina 28 -70mm ATX zoom lens, f/16 at 2 secs. Tripod. Photo by Lynda Harper. Fuji Velvia responds well to greens – as you can see here. By using a slow shutter speed and her camera set on a sturdy tripod, Lynda has enabled the water to flow through this beautiful scene with a fine sense of movement.

CASTLE HILL IN WINTER
Fujichrome 50 Professional, Mamiya 645 Super with 35mm wide-angle lens, f/16 at 1/250 sec.
Seasonal changes always bring new opportunities for the photographer. Freshly fallen snow sparkles in the soft sunlight and blue shadows. If you're shooting into the sun – as I am here – watch out for flare. Remove all filters and shade the lens if you can – use either a lens hood or a hat.

snow-capped mountain or still reeds by the lakeside. If you are photographing floating water plants, which can be a most attractive subject, try using a polarising filter at right angles to the sun to bring out the colour and detail of both the leaves and water, then try shooting the plant leaves into the sun, using the reflected sunlight to transform the floating leaves into silvery motes dancing on the water. In the latter case, you will need to underexpose by at least one stop.

Anything moving across water, be it a bird or boat, or merely the wind, will create interesting ripples and can strengthen the power of an image. Any movement, however slight, will distort anything reflected in water, so that a sunlit forest of green trees becomes a medley of coloured shapes in the water; and the sun or moon becomes, not a sphere, but a vibrant stairway of light.

Mist, fog and haze

Mists and fogs are magically ephemeral things for the photographer to work with. If you like evocative, misty pictures – and who doesn't? – then rising early before the sun and wind is well worth the effort. As you can see from one or two images in this book, fog and mist are things that I greatly enjoy personally. Again, watch for very rapid light and mood changes with fog and in lifting mists. And watch out for condensation on your lenses and your camera's viewfinder window.

Tripods and the wind

The tripod is undoubtedly the landscape photographer's best friend. With it, you can lower the camera's point of view and use the tremendous depth of field of your wide-angle lens. The scene rolls away, pin sharp, from near your feet to the distant hills.

A breeze is a nuisance to the landscape photographer. With slow film, a slow shutter speed, great depth of field, a tripod and a cable release, all ought to go well – unless a capricious wind is blowing. Under these conditions, anything that moves will blur, how much depending on how big the subject is, and how close it is to the camera. If you are faced with a fitful breeze, set your camera up, hold the cable release in your hand, then watch the scene closely. When there is a momentary lull, click. This often requires great patience. Try for landscapes early in the morning before a wind springs up. On the other hand, wind can sometimes enhance the photographic qualities of a landscape, like the blurred motion a breeze creates in a field of wheat, or in a nodding throng of flowers. Try a few pictures and see.

People in landscapes

If you use people in your landscape pictures, they should be integrated carefully into a scene, so that they don't look as though they've been thrown into it. While the farmer and his handiwork form a vital part of country lore, avoid the trappings of civilization, such as cars, buses, filling stations, trash cans, or rubbish and conspicuous power lines, unless you deliberately want to include them. While I know some modern photographers concentrate on environmental issues by creating images reeking of dead animals, trash and pollution – and have my admiration for doing so – each of us must decide what we want our images to express. I prefer to let the natural landscape, free from human interference, speak through my pictures. It is becoming harder and harder to achieve this in many countries of the world.

THE FORGOTTEN GATE
Fuji Velvia 50, Canon EOS 10 with Sigma 21 - 35mm zoom lens, f/16 at 1/15 sec.
Tripod. Photo by Lynda Harper.
The hay lies ready for removal from the fields, but this forgotten gate, and its retinue of fence-line weeds, lies seemingly abandoned. The composition is helped by the parallel lines of hay and the contrast in colour between the warm earth and cool sky.

LAKE MATHESON

Fuji Velvia 50, Mamiya 645 Super with 80mm macro lens, pola filter. Tripod.
The dark waters of the brooding lake are still, streaks of cirrus cloud brighten up the sky, and a wash of sunlight illuminates the forest in the middle ground. We were ready for New Zealand's most famous lake, and on this early August morning, it was ready for us. Mount Tasman on the left, Mount Cook on the right.

THE UNEXPECTED CALLER
Kodachrome. Photo by George Chance.
This sensitive shot of a wild deer was taken at Nara in Japan. George has carefully framed the animal with beautifully textured stone lanterns. Being ready for the unexpected is the key to wildlife photography.

Landscapes offer a vast treasury of wildlife for photographers – gnarled trees creaking with the years, delicate ferns, fragrant flowers, multi-coloured fungi, and marvellous creatures, both large and small. For wildlife photographers, auto-focusing lenses have been a great stride forward in obtaining sharply focused images quickly and easily.

Photographing animals

Start with animals you know. Photographing your pet will require a short telephoto lens. The AF 100mm or 105mm is ideal, because its magnification (double the standard 50mm lens) produces photographs that draw the viewer's eye to the subject. Lenses of this focal length also provide a natural perspective and a shallow depth of field. An excellent lens with which to begin taking portraits of flowers and animals.

Understanding animals

This is essential, and with pets it's easy, because you already have the animal's confidence. Put your camera on a tripod, design your picture carefully, check your focusing and depth-of-field, make certain your shutter speed is fast enough to stop any blurring, wait for the right moment, and take the picture. Bracket your exposures to ensure that at least some will be correctly exposed. Take notes on what you took and how. If your camera has spot metering, take a careful reading of your subject first. This is especially important in those instances where you have say, a black animal sitting in bright sunlight which will create exposure problems.

Remember that AF cameras can now routinely cope with a lot of unusual lighting, but some earlier camera lightmeters cannot.

EYE OF A DOLPHIN
Fujichrome 100 Professional, Nikon F 801 with Nikkor 180-mm lens, f/5.6 at 1/250 sec.
Seven wild dolphins swam up to our vessel and gave us the eye. This image proved to me that autofocus cameras can successfully focus on a defined subject under the surface of the water. It was on that 1989 field trip that I became convinced of the true worth of AF cameras. Twenty-five years of manually focusing everything disappeared in the twinkle of that dolphin's eye.

A black animal and a bright background will create problems of correct exposure. You can have one or the other correctly exposed, but not both. To achieve this you will need to reduce the contrast between the black subject and its bright background. A cloudy day or open shade will give you a much more pleasing picture. I suggest that you use a fairly fast film, something like Fujichrome or Ektachrome 100 ISO, or even faster, such as Kodachrome 200 ISO. Incidentally, if you photograph your pets under artificial light, the pictures will have an orange cast over them. Daylight colour film in general use is balanced for sunlight, so it is best to use a flash unit when photographing anything indoors.

Wild animals

Visit your library and read all you can about the animal you are interested in. Ask people who know animals well for assistance. If visiting a reserve or other area where many and various animals occur, take time out to acquaint yourself with as many as you can. Become familiar with, and respectful of, an animal's needs and behaviour. Ideally you should go and live with them, in their natural surroundings. It's no accident that animal researchers usually take the best conceived and most interesting images of the animals they're studying.

Most animals have predictable behaviour. They have specific places where they like to eat, rest and sleep. Shags will roost in the same grove of trees, a mouse will shelter in the same old shoe for weeks at a time, and many seabirds leave their nests in burrows to fly thousands of kilometres about the oceans only to return with unerring accuracy to the same burrow year after year. Even limpets have their favourite crevices. All this is good news for the photographer. You can plan to return when the light is right and the animal is at home. Indeed, you may know, quite accurately, when a migratory animal will return to its place of birth.

Most wild animals have acute senses of sight, smell and hearing because they rely on these senses to survive. Predators seldom give them a second chance. Remember this when stalking an animal. Do not travel upwind of any creature with a wet nose, because it will smell you long before you come within camera range. Don't make eye contact with an animal as this often will alarm it. Above all, never approach an animal in such a way that you block its escape route. Seals, for example, take an extremely dim view of humans who come between themselves and the sea and some species, such as bull fur seals and sea-lions, are aggressive and can move surprisingly quickly on land.

The old trick of approaching an animal openly and slowly in a zigzag manner, while pretending to gaze intently at the ground, works well. Animals feel much more secure if they can clearly see you advancing. These manoeuvres take time, so make sure you have plenty of it. And it's a good idea to preset the anticipated f/stop and shutter speed. And don't forget to have your AF lens set on autofocus. I once watched a learned wildlife photographer spend nearly two hours stalking a bird with a big telephoto lens. He had a 1600 ISO film and all the equipment. But he forgot the autofocus switch on his lens. He stood up, shot a heap of film and then realised that his lens was still manually focused on two metres. The bird flew away, probably laughing.

Once within range, you should raise the camera slowly to your eye. Remember long lenses can look ominous to shy creatures. Sudden reflections can also startle even large animals, which can create rapid action even more exciting than you bargained for.

Respect your subjects

Some animals which have had little dealings with humans, are quite curious, and will approach you closely. The Emperor Penguins of Antarctica are fearless and totally captivating creatures and will allow you to come near to them. They probably figure that you're a somewhat bigger example of them. Smaller species of polar penguin, however, react rather differently. These birds can be pugnacious, and will attack your legs with the clear intention of harming them. In so doing, however, the birds may inadvertently expose their eggs to predation by the rapacious skua (a large, gull-like

***BENGAL TIGER** (**Panthera tigris**)*
Photo by M.L. Peck/D.R. Fernandez.
Tigers are magnificent and photogenic beasts to see at any time. Focus on their eyes and fill the frame with either a head shot, or the complete animal. Be careful.

GREAT BLUE HERON (Ardea herodias) FEEDING ON MARINE IGUANA HATCHLING AT FERNANDINA ISLAND, GALAPAGOS.

Photo by Tui De Roy. Nikon camera. No further details. When stalking wildlife keep your telephoto lens on autofocus, your camera set on focus tracking, and the shutter capable to fire off several frames in quick succession. I find f/5.6 is a good general f/stop for aperture priority, so that the camera will select the corresponding shutter speed, but you might prefer to use shutter priority, and let the camera set the f/stop. Whatever you decide, be prepared for anything. Try to anticipate from which direction your quarry might launch into flight – this will allow a few extra shots before it's gone. And, if you have now nearly exhausted your film, you might decide to load a fresh 36 exposure cartridge in your camera before setting off again. Otherwise, Murphy's Law will catch you without any instantly available film.

predator), which will steal penguin eggs to eat. They are a rich source of food and easily obtained when the parent birds are distracted.

I mention this because many tourists are now visiting Antarctic penguins in their natural habitat, and any careless approach by large numbers of people can not only disturb them, but can also cause the loss of their eggs and chicks. This little example raises an important point that I cannot stress enough – respect animals – remember you are the intruder. The animal's welfare must always be more important than your piece of film. Take extraordinary care when photographing wildlife.

Composition with AF lenses

Cameras that autofocus on subjects dead centre in the frame are going to give you an image that can appear static and boring. Some cameras, however, autofocus in small areas or sections off-centre and will usually light up the one they're operating on. This is extremely helpful for improving the composition of an image. However, if you can select only the right or left hand autofocus marker, this will still allow you considerable flexibility to craft a more interesting image of wildlife than those cameras without such features. If you are a wildlife fanatic, check these features in any new camera very carefully.

Make sure that when using such AF markers that you keep them fully on your target at all times, until you are ready to take the picture. This will require concentration, manipulative skill and plenty of practice. I would anticipate major developments from the camera-makers in giving us freedom in the near future to selectively autofocus anywhere in the frame.

Telephoto lenses

Telephoto lenses are bread-and-butter lenses for the wildlife photographer. They range up to 2000mm in focal length with the large ones being both heavy and fearsomely expensive.

The AF 300mm f/2.8 lens is an expensive optic, but with a 2x extender it becomes a 600mm f/5.6 – a useful combination for a wildlife photographer. Together they weigh about 3kg (6lb 9oz) – half that of the 6kg (13lb 2oz) AF 600mm f/4 prime lens. This lens has a price tag that will bring tears to your eyes.

If, however, you are seriously intent on wildlife/bird photography you will need a fast 400mm or a 600mm AF lens, together with a substantial tripod and the equipment to build a hide. This decision will cost you a lot of money, but it will enable you to close in on distant or small subjects that would otherwise be extremely difficult, if not impossible, to photograph.

'Wait and see' photography

I prefer to travel relatively light; I will hunt down my picture rather than stake it out. Other photographers hide and wait – sometimes for hours. 'Wait and see' photography offers great rewards, and suitable places to hide can be built of handy natural materials, or can be more elaborate. The choice is yours. One of my friends uses a wardrobe which he painted green and drilled two holes in it – one for an eye and the other for his camera lens! The great green wardrobe currently resides in his garden – I would hate to see the day he decides to take it somewhere else.

A hide serves to conceal you from your subject, and if you are constructing it near a bird's nest, or animal's den, remember to build it in stages to avoid alarming your subjects. Each day, as your hide takes shape, bring it a little closer. For small birds such as finches, the hide in its final position should be about 2.5 m (just over 8 feet) away from the subject. A 200mm lens is ideal. For larger creatures the hide can be more distant. A nest is not the only place for a hide; try a drinking hole, or a place where food is abundant – perhaps a muddy lake shore where animals congregate. Once inside your hide, you're ready to 'wait and see'.

Habitat shots

Until you buy a big telephoto lens which allows you to fill the frame with the animal you wish to photograph, your 70 - 210mm or 80 -200mm zoom lens can be used effectively for pictures showing animals within their natural habitat.

Habitat pictures are extremely important, and far too many people ignore them in the race to get an animal portrait. Never neglect habitat shots, because they are

GREATER FLAMINGOES (Phoenicopterus ruber) COURTSHIP DISPLAY, JERVIS ISLAND, GALAPAGOS.
Photo by Tui De Roy.
This image works not only for the unusual nature of the subject, but also because the beautiful light has thrown the birds into strong contrast with the dark background. Lighting your subject in this way is a powerful means to make a strong image. Note, too, how the photographer has made good use of the available space.

BURCHELL'S ZEBRA (Equus burchelli), ETOSHA NATIONAL PARK, NAMIBIA.
Photo by D.R. Fernandez/M.L. Peck.
Beautiful side lighting on these zebra at a water hole has created a very fine shot. Early morning and late afternoon light is often the best for many animals – it is also a time when they are most active.

particularly valuable in illustrating where an animal lives. In fact, if you are showing your wildlife pictures to friends, or giving a lecture on the subject, your audience will expect to see habitat pictures before they see your close-ups. Habitat and portrait pictures go together; they complement each other. They are fundamental to telling a good visual story about the animals or plants that you are discussing.

Habitat pictures require good composition, and because you may not necessarily be close enough to the animal to alarm it, take time out to consider all the elements of good pictorial design and where you wish to place the animal within your frame. Otherwise you will get a rather poor record, which will have merit only if the animal is unusual or rare. Try to get the animal looking into the picture rather than out of it and avoid shooting it on the shadow side unless you want its silhouette.

Many small, cold-blooded creatures such as snakes and lizards emerge early in the day to bask in the sun, warming their bodies sufficiently to become highly mobile and ready to forage. Until they're warm and active they tend to be lethargic and are relatively easy subjects to photograph. Stroking the belly of some skinks and small lizards puts them into a stupor from which they need a few minutes to recover – just enough time to get a few shots in, before the animal comes to, and scuttles away.

Animal portraits

Good animal portraits should give you a detailed view of an animal's appearance so that you are able to count the number of whiskers on a chin, or the number of feathers in a tail. Portraits of this type are thus useful in positively confirming the identity of any unknown creature.

An animal portrait needs to be well exposed with high definition. The old axiom 'always make sure you get the eyes sharp' is a very good rule-of-thumb for animal photography. Focus on the eyes, then check with your depth-of-field preview button to ensure that the remainder of the face is sharp. This care in focusing is particularly important if a creature has a long nose or a big bill. Your camera's autofocus lock button can be very handy in situations such as this.

An animal that is long in the body, such as a snake, lizard, or even a seal, can generate focusing problems for the photographer, because it is usually difficult to get the head and the rest of the body sharply in focus at the same time. If you are unable to get the whole body on a flat plane relative to the camera, which minimises focusing problems, you can either drop most of the body out of the picture, relying on closure to complete it, or try to get a close-up of the head in the same way as we take a head-and-shoulders portrait.

Birds on the wing

If you wish to photograph birds flying about close to you in a consistent pattern, such as those following a ship or wheeling about near their nests, autofocusing means that you can effectively follow them about and merely wait for the right moment to take the picture. Some slower AF lenses may have trouble keeping up with the birds and you should not attach tele-extenders on to lenses when doing this, as they slow down the lens's ability to focus even further. Some may not even focus at all. A good one for aerial seabird photography would be an AF 300mm f/2.8 lens. Use a fast film and hand hold the camera. Yes, I've actually seen people set up tripods on a vessel at sea. Amazing !

Wildlife on snow or sand

Most modern AF electronic cameras can cope rather well with difficult lighting problems such as snow or having the sun in the field of view. If your photographs taken on matrix metering come out well – with the white snow looking white and not grey – then you will know that your camera can cope with these conditions without any adjustment to the lightmeter readings. Check these things carefully before you go on an expensive safari.

Some older camera lightmeters, however, are not calibrated to handle bright snow or white sand, and will invariably struggle to underexpose these pictures. It may seem strange with so much light about that your pictures appear too dark, but this is because the lightmeter wants to reduce everything to the industry's standard neutral grey card with an 18 per cent reflectance. It does not understand that you want everything to be pristine white. As a consequence, you will need to over expose deliberately by one stop under snowy conditions. You can either set your exposure compensation dial to +1, slow down the ISO rating of your film, or make the changes manually to your shutter speed dial and aperture settings. Remember to bracket your exposures – whether you have the latest model camera or an older one.

A white bird on a dark background

This is another trap for the inexperienced photographer, again because of some lightmeters' preference for grey. You may, for example, want to photograph a white gull sitting on its nest among a swathe of green and grey foliage. If the bird tends to be small in the overall picture it will be over exposed, because the lightmeter, in the main, sees the dark background and does not take enough account of the white bird that you want to expose correctly. You need to expose for the bird and not the background. Spot metering on many modern AF cameras is excellent for this.

If, however, you cannot approach closely without disturbing the bird, and decide to put a telephoto lens on the camera and take the reading from the gull using the magnified image the telephoto lens gives you, you will get underexposure. Allow more light on to the film, otherwise your exposure will be for a grey bird instead of a white one.

Most birds wisely avoid approaching humans. It is pointless seeking birds in anything other than clothes that blend in with your surroundings. You can generate some interesting pictures in which blur creates a feeling of rapid movement by using a relatively slow shutter speed.

DURBAR SQUARE, KATHMANDU

Fujichrome 100 Professional, Mamiya 645 Super, with 35mm wide-angle lens, f/5.6 at 1/125 sec. Hand held.

Wide-angle lenses have wonderful story-telling potential as you can see. Note the babe in the basket and the crutches. Short focal-length lenses mean that we can use fairly slow shutter speeds without the danger of camera shake. Use a relatively fast film and be up early to catch the action. Overcast days minimize heavy shadows and bring the colours to life. People don't have to squint. Ask permission from the people you wish to photograph.

SEEDS
Society. London
KATHMANDU
AVAILABLE
HERE

Close-up photography usually requires a considerable amount of time, so plan your itinerary accordingly. Take a close-up lens if you are visiting a place in the spring or summer when alpine flowers will be in bloom or if you are a close-up buff who cannot live without your close-up lens. You might consider taking your 50 - 60mm macro lens for exotic flowers, beetles, or close-ups of ancient hieroglyphs and the like. If you have a 100mm or 105mm f/2.8 macro lens, you could take it along together with a 2x converter. This would give you a sharp 200mm f/5.6 lens, which should be adequate for most general telephoto requirements.

Film

I suggest that you take two, maybe three, types of film. For landscapes and close-ups use Fuji's excellent 50 ISO Velvia film. Fujichrome 100 ISO, pushed to 200 ISO gives excellent, if slightly warmer, results. I've used it extensively and find it excellent for travel photography, particularly with subjects in heavy shade or interior shots of interesting buildings. Remember that when you push a film you must override its DX coding and ensure that the entire film is shot off at 200 ISO. Mark all such films clearly so that your processing laboratory knows what to do (push ONE) when they come to develop it. For wildlife photography you could take some 400 ISO film. Most of these can be pushed to 800 ISO (push ONE) if poor lighting conditions or the speed of the animals warrant it. Extremely fast film in the 1000 ISO category can catch the excitement of fast action that slower films would undoubtedly miss. There's nothing wrong with a sharp – if grainy shot – of a lion trying to catch a fly sitting on its nose.

THE NEVER-ENDING STORY

Fujichrome 100 pushed to 200, Canon EOS 10, with Canon 28-80mm L zoom lens, f/5.6 at 1/250 sec. Hand held.
Fujichrome pushed to 200 is ideal for grab shots and I couldn't resist the gentle humour of this one. Such images add sparkle to our travel photography. Note the composition: an ellipse of dogs and sticks, a wall of squares and triangles, and the strong shapes of the tree and the monkey. The latter help balance off the seated, human figures.

What I took to Nepal and China

For a recent 28-day photographic study tour to Nepal and Guilin with 14 students, I took the following gear:

1 Canon EOS 10 body and two lenses: a 20 - 35mm f/2.8 L zoom and a 28 - 80 f/2.8-f/4 L zoom; with a 72-mm polarising filter to fit both of these; and a Canon 430 EZ flash.

1 Leica R5 camera body with two Leica lenses: one 60mm f/2.8 macro lens and a 180mm f/3.4 APO telephoto lens together with a 2x extender.

Accessories included a spare cable release, a small reflector board (for close-up photography: see later chapter); a graduated grey filter and several spare battery sets.

Film: 30 rolls of Fuji Velvia 50 ISO; 20 rolls of Fujichrome Professional 100 ISO film and two rolls each of Fuji 800/1600/3200 ISO ultra high speed film. (I know some so-called professional photographers who proudly announce that they shoot hundreds of rolls of film when out on assignment – it seems to me that they need some real help with their photography !).

The above combination of equipment worked well. I took my own advice and picked my shots carefully. The result was 25 rolls of exposed film: 20 taken with the Canon, and 5 on the Leica. Most of the Fujichrome 100 ISO was pushed to 200 ISO. The ultra-fast film was shot at 1600 ISO with the Leica and a 180mm lens during a five-hour trip up the Li River in the Guilin province of China. The Canon AF camera worked beautifully for just about everything: people, landscapes and interiors with flash. It was quick and easy – a delight to use. I used the 20-35mm lens twice, all my remaining shots were taken with the 28 - 80mm L lens with pushed Fuji 100 ISO film. I found the electronic remote which triggered the EOS 10 camera from a distance of up to three or four metres very useful.

The Leica and the 1600 ISO film enabled me to shoot from the boat Guilin landscapes at very fast shutter speeds and to obtain very grainy but extremely interesting images – something I plan to explore much more fully in future. I did not use the 2x extender during our trip. The Leica and the macro lens enabled me to shoot several close-ups of the early spring flowers of Nepal on the slow Fuji Velvia film. I found the two camera bodies worked well in tandem, enabling me to use most effectively my three films of different speeds.

Next time I go overseas I'll take two cameras again. I have replaced all my Leica gear with two Canon EOS 5s and several Canon L zoom lenses. The quality of the modern generation zoom lenses is something that I scarcely would have believed possible a few years ago.

Some do's and don'ts to remember

NEVER go overseas with the idea of buying your camera somewhere duty-free or for a cheaper price than you can buy it at home. You must be thoroughly familiar with your camera before you go. Travel is such a full-time occupation that there will not be time for you to learn how to be proficient with any new camera.

Buy your new camera at least three months before you go. Put enough film through it to check that everything works properly, and that you feel completely confident with it. For instance, suppose you find yourself in Hong Kong and want to take a shot of the city at night. How would you do it? Find out now: before you go.

Make sure that all your equipment will fit under the airline's seat. Put your tripod

THE EVERLASTING EYES OF COMPASSION
Fujichrome 100 pushed to 200, Canon EOS 10, with Canon 28-80mm L zoom lens, f/8 at 1/250 sec. Tripod.
This colourful image of the golden Buddhist stupa and its fluttering prayer flags at Swayambhunath, atop a green hill, in Kathmandu, Nepal, is beautifully set off by the blue background of the morning sky. An ancient, and much revered site, over 2500 years old, it is certainly not to be missed if you are visiting Nepal.

in the overhead locker. They can be damaged going through with general luggage – even when it is in a bag. One of our tripods sent through with our bags received a severe crease in one of its legs so that it couldn't be extended properly. Someone's suitcase had obviously been thrown on top of it. One way to avoid this is to wrap your tripod in a sheet of bubble plastic-wrap and secure this with several large rubber bands before placing it into the tripod case. Thus packed, all our other tripods survived the long journey from New Zealand-Bangkok-Kathmandu-China-Hong Kong and home again without sustaining any damage whatsoever.

If you do feel confident enough to buy an expensive piece of equipment overseas, always buy something that is brand new, with the factory seal intact. Never buy a used item from a display case. Some of these veterans can sweat it out for months under the constant heat of interior display lights or sunlight. The temperature in such enclosed places can liquefy the grease in lenses, allowing this to flow on to the diaphragm blades thus rendering them, and the lens, totally useless.

Check the equipment carefully before you put a foot outside the shop. The condition of the box will be a good indication of just how long any item has been sitting on the shelf. Some manufacturers begin their serial numbers with the year of manufacture e.g. 94xxxx for 1994. Make sure that you get an international guarantee card and that it is properly filled out before you leave the premises.

Always take all the film that you will need with you. Unscrupulous souls in some countries will fill a cassette with used film, carefully seal up the film carton again and sell you the result as new unexposed film. Yes, it still happens, and it could happen to you.

If you are travelling to a damp moist place, carry your gear in plastic bags with silica gel as a drying agent. Make sure that you regularly dry the silica gel in order for it to do its job efficiently.

Never adorn your camera bag with badges or labels that advertise the fact that the contents are worth stealing. Be sensible: remove all manufacturer's decals – anything that might indicate an expensive camera lies within. Avoid those flashy neck straps which advertise your camera preference. Thieves know what you've got and can steal to order.

Keep both exposed and unexposed film as cool as you can. Nothing kills film faster than too much tropical heat. Hotel security safes are usually cool and safe. Put your camera gear in the hotel's security safe when you are not using it. Especially at night.

I hand-carry all my film in a clear plastic bag or container so that it can be easily inspected by custom officials. Never put them in your luggage. That is just asking for trouble. A handy cassette or two of a particularly fast film (1600 ISO) in your pocket can be winningly helpful in persuading some recalcitrant customs officials to inspect all your film by hand.

That said, don't get paranoid about the small, airport X-ray machines that reveal the contents of your hand luggage which you carry with you when boarding a plane. If your film is rated under 500 ISO you have nothing to worry about. I've had films X-rayed many times with no problems whatsoever. It's in every country's best interests to ensure that their visitors' films don't get damaged by their X-ray machines.

ANCIENT CORRIDORS OF TIME FORGOTTEN
Fujichrome 100, Nikon FA with Nikkor 20mm wide-angle lens, f/11 at 1/30 sec. Hand held. Photo by Lynda Harper. This image creaks with age and reeks with atmosphere. The human figure, and the strong lines of perspective leading to her add compositional strength to this image within the holiest of Hindu shrines at Pashupatinath, Nepal.

At the end of each photographic foray, carefully check all your gear to ensure that everything has been returned to its rightful place. This will avoid you leaving a cable release behind, or that expensive polarising filter you took off and put down... somewhere.

If you are visiting the polar region, or where air temperatures get very cold at night, remember that colour films can snap in half if you're not careful with them. While the newer emulsions give greater detail and contrast, they are also thinner than the older film types that you may be familiar with. The new films can snap surprisingly easily when made brittle by cold dry air.

High temperatures can also soften film emulsion, making it easy to tear. In such places rewind your film by hand – if your camera allows you to (as opposed to power-winding it back into the cassette). Saves battery power, too.

Bring your exposed film home for processing. Don't be tempted into letting someone you don't know develop all those great shots that have taken your life savings and all your holiday time to obtain. Some countries develop their films with colour differences that they like, but you might not.

Make sure that your travel insurance covers all the countries that you are likely to visit and that it covers the full duration of your travelling.

Some tips

Approach your subjects in a creative manner and avoid commonplace objects that have long ago lost their novelty and their ability to excite. The identity of the subject need not be important: it is how it is created – not what it is.

Travel by yourself if you can (tour buses will always pass your best creative shots and land you with the dull and boring masterpieces that everyone has taken before).

Concentrate on what you're doing – really look at what you want to photograph, and have patience. A few minutes will determine whether something is going to happen or not.

Two final points

Remember– Murphy's Law's favourite time to strike is when you are on holiday, in a strange and unfamiliar place, having the time of your life. Be alert and be careful.

MORNING LIGHT CARESS FOR THE TAJ MAHAL
Fujichrome 100, Olympus OM 4Ti, with Zuiko 24mm lens, f/4 at 1/125 sec. Hand held. Photo by Bevan Tulett.
Bevan was there when the side-lighting was perfect for this subject and before the jostling crowds arrived. Because 24mm wide-angle lenses have such a wide depth-of-field, they can be hand-held down to quite slow shutter speeds without losing detail sharpness. The symmetry, the depth, the delicate hues of colour, the reflections, and the glorious repose in this image makes it especially attractive.

And, as a caring photographer, be alive to the cultural sensitivities of your host country before you arrive there. If in any doubt, always politely ask if you may take a photograph. Not to do so is just plain bad manners.

BIRD'S NEST FUNGI GROWING ON OLD ROPE
Fuji Velvia, Leica R5 with 100mm APO macro lens, f/16 at 1 sec. Tripod.
An interesting subject and careful attention to composition has resulted in this image. Don't use autofocusing for your macro photography. Take your time and focus manually. Check your depth-of-field carefully before making the picture.

Of all the realms of photographing nature none gives me as much pleasure as close-up photography. A small part of the forest floor, or an alpine meadow, can keep me spellbound for hours. It's a magical journey, which, once made, you'll want to return to again and again.

Taking close-ups is a relatively simple procedure to learn. You need:

1. The right equipment.
2. An understanding of depth-of-field and the importance of correct focusing.
3. An appreciation of how to light something close to the camera.

Equipment

Modern autofocus cameras are well suited to macro photography because you can see plainly what lies within the frame before you take the picture, and the camera's lightmeter reading systems allow for precise measurements to be made of the light levels for well-exposed pictures.

The most important piece of equipment for the close-up photographer is undoubtedly the lens. Most major camera manufacturers make what are called macro or micro lenses designed for close-up work, and more and more people are finding the joys that these lenses offer them. Zoom lenses with close-focusing facilities seldom produce as good close-up pictures because, despite all the advertising hype, no manufacturer has contrived a zoom lens that will do absolutely everything.

Macro (Nikon refers to them as 'micro') lenses usually come in three groups of focal lengths; 50 or 60mm, 90 to 105mm, and 200mm. The new generation of macro lenses allow full (life-size) reproduction without any tube attachments or supplementary lenses, and this makes them extremely handy and quick to use. For other macro lenses

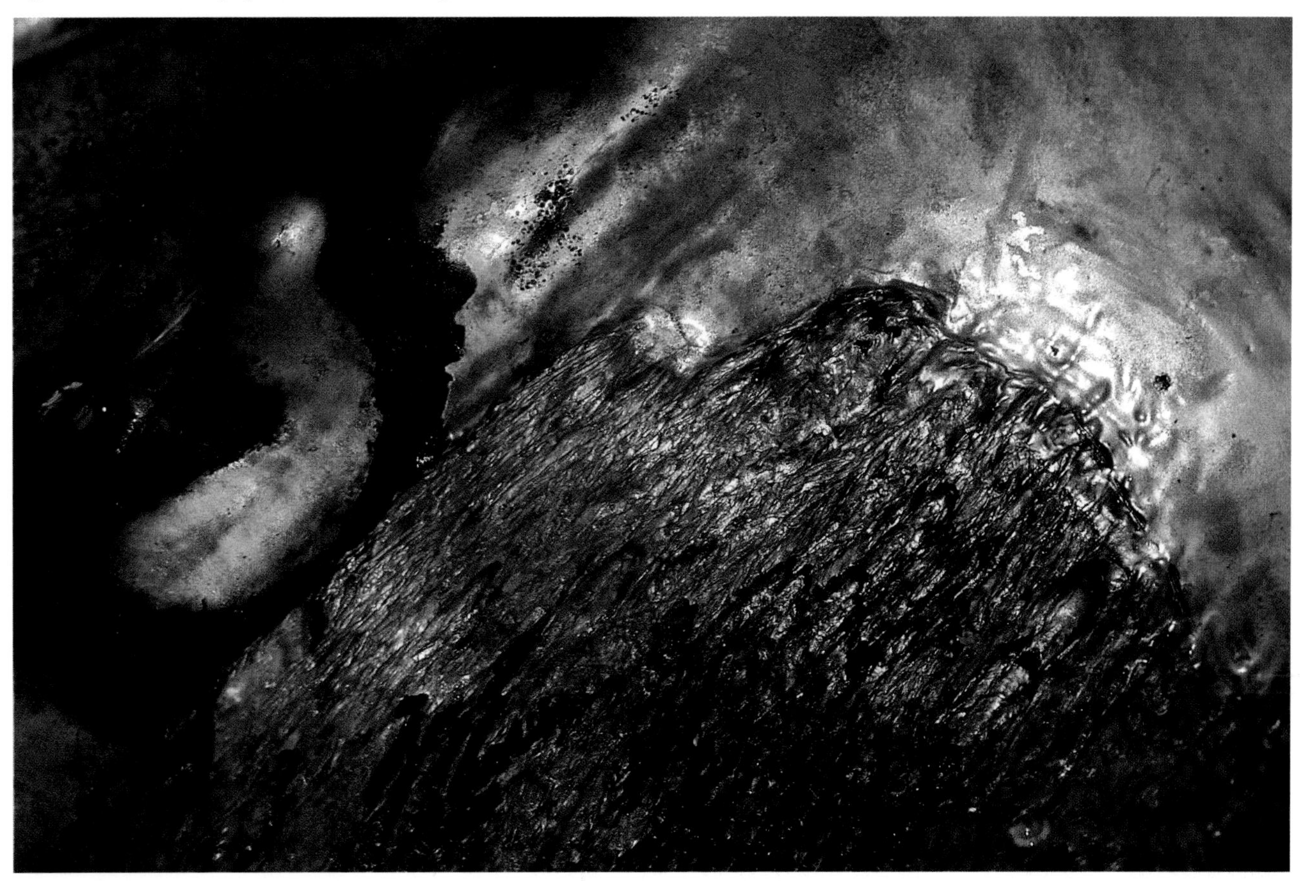

A WET PAUA (ABALONE) SHELL

Fuji Velvia, Leica R5 with 100mm APO macro lens, f/22 at 2 secs. Tripod.
The wonderful colour and detail attracted me to this macro shot. This image was taken with the lens at full extension - 1:1 (life-size) - and shows that even at f/22 I had only a few millimetres depth-of-field.

COLOUR AND ICE
Fuji Velvia. Nikon FA with Tokina 90mm ATX macro lens. f/16 at 2 secs.
Photo by Lynda Harper.
The ice and the mosses have combined to produce a joyous feast for the eye. Note the good use of available space here. If you close your eyes slightly you will see that shape and size of the dark areas in this image agreeably balance each other out. When framing up your images, this is a good thing to do.

it is possible to buy a matching automatic extension ring that allows you to obtain the 1:1 (life-size) reproduction ratio should you need it.

Macro lenses are more expensive than the standard lens of the same focal length because they are premium optics with excellent characteristics. They have a relatively slow maximum aperture, but this is of little relevance to the macro photographer, who prefers good sharpness, high contrast, and a great depth-of-field for their chosen field of photography. Macro lenses are designed to close down to a small minimum aperture such as f/32, which is very useful where a maximum zone of sharpness is required. This is not always the case, however. There will be many times when a larger aperture allows you to block off a distracting background by effectively blurring it.

Autofocusing your macros

Don't. Autofocusing is great for most things but not for close-up photography. Why? Because most often where you want to achieve critical focus may not be where the AF macro lens wants to focus. Correct focusing at ultra-close range is vital because the depth-of-field is very shallow. Therefore manually focus every time, very carefully, particularly if you are using larger apertures such as f/4 or f/5.6 where the zone of sharpness may only be a few millimetres.

An example. A 100mm macro lens at 2:1 offers a depth-of-field of only 1.6mm at f/2.8 and about 12.4mm at f/22. If you focus even closer, to lifesize, (1:1) the depth-of-field is reduced to only 0.6mm at f/2.8, and only 4.7mm at f/22. Now you know why focusing is so important! Check your macro lens instruction sheet and find out exactly how much depth-of-field you have to work with.

So remember, use your AF macro lens, but just turn off the autofocusing. The lens-makers are well aware of this procedure, and usually supply large rubber focusing grips to help you manually focus your lens easily and with accuracy. You will also notice that most AF macro lenses have a switch for limited and full focusing ranges. This saves battery power when your lens has to wind in and out over a wide focusing range. By all means use your macro lens for general photography on autofocus, but for anything very close it is best to turn it off.

Note: If you use a manually focusing macro lens on your AF camera you may lose some lightmetering and some fill-in flash opportunities that are only available if you use an electronically compatible camera and lenses.

Close-ups with the 50/60mm macro lenses

If you buy a 50mm or 60mm AF or manual macro lens and focus on something close to the camera, one thing will become obvious immediately. You'll find the lens barrel ending up only a few centimetres from your subject. This is fine for a subject that doesn't mind having an enormous alien object very close to it, but most living things, such as insects, will either flee or hide as fast as they can. You will also notice that with the 50/60mm macro lens fully extended, the subject can become deformed owing to the accentuated perspective of the lens.

ALPINE FLOWERS

Fuji Velvia, Leica R 5, with 35mm lens, f/16 at 2 secs. Tripod.

An image of New Zealand's beautiful giant buttercup ***Ranunculus lyalli*** *in flower. When photographing flowers, try to vary your shots, and make sure that you include at least one showing the flowers in their natural setting. Wind is the usual problem of photographing alpine flowers. Pick your day if you can – early morning is best – or use some sort of wind block if you can't – your back-pack, a friend, an umbrella, a hat. Remember that your depth-of-field may only be a few millimetres in extent, so try to get your flowers on the same plane as your film. Reduce undue contrast by either using a small reflector board or some fill-in flash. Watch your exposure with white flowers. Ask yourself whether your camera's computer can compensate by over-exposing slightly or will you need to over-expose by about 2/3rds of a stop yourself in order to retain the white of the flower's petals? Bracket your exposures to be sure.*

ENCHANTED MOSS
Fujichrome 50 Professional, Nikon FA with Tokina 90mm ATX macro lens. f16 at 30 secs. Tripod. Photo by Lynda Harper.
In the close-up world the ordinary can become extraordinary. By using a small reflector board, Lynda was able to beam sunlight into this beautiful macro image, so bringing it vividly to life. Reflector boards are easy to make and are valuable tools to enliven your macro photography.

Being very close to your subject creates another problem – one of lighting. Being cheek by jowl with your subject means that you will often find the camera shading it. What to do with the light can be tricky, particularly if your small subject decides to walk away while you are photographing it with a one-second exposure.

The 90 to 105mm macro lenses

The major camera manufacturers and the independent lens makers each produce macro lenses within the 90 to 105mm range. If you are seriously interested in close-up photography, I strongly recommend buying one of these focal length autofocus macro lens made by your camera-maker. They are rather expensive but well worth saving for. Because of their natural perspective characteristics and excellent performance, these lenses are not only ideal for close-up work but are also excellent for general photography. With such lenses the working distance is about twice that of the 50/60mm standard or macro lens and this also allows the use of reflector boards or flash to solve problems of low light and camera shadowing.

If you have a manually operating camera, look no further than the Tokina 90mm AT-X f/2.5 macro lens, which I used for many years for most of my close-up work. It comes in most mounts and has a high optical performance. It's easy to use and the f/2.5 maximum aperture allows more light into the viewfinder for easier focusing than some slower macro lenses in the same focal length. Given that the Tokina is also cheaper than its leading brand equivalents, I can recommend it unreservedly to you. Tokina have produced a new AF 100mm f/2.8 lens which, if it is anything like its predecessor, should be an excellent optic.

Alternatives to macro lenses

Can't afford a macro lens just yet? Then try close-up supplementary lenses that screw on to the front of your existing lenses. They're reasonably cheap and a good way to begin exploring macro photography. Supplementary close-up lenses come in varying strengths, and effectively reduce the minimum focusing distance, so increasing the magnification of your prime lens. Most of the camera functions – including autofocusing – are maintained. Because they come only in certain sizes, make sure that they fit your lens first, and buy only those made by your camera or lens manufacturer. Avoid screwing supplementary lenses on to zoom lenses – fit them to the best optic that you have in order to obtain best results.

FROSTED FOLIAGE
Fujichrome 100, Nikon F4 with Tokina 90mm macro lens, f/16 at 1 sec. Tripod. Photo by Paul Kennedy.
The soft light and careful attention to composition has resulted in this very pleasing shot. The dark background helps to throw the subject into bold relief.

The same applies to extension tubes. You might have an expensive telephoto lens that is the wrong fitting-size for supplementary lenses. Extension tubes fit at the other end of the lens – between it and the camera body and allow a much greater magnification of your subject than do supplementary lenses. Modern extension tubes retain all the electrical contacts to ensure that nothing is lost by fitting them. Manual focusing is a must when using extension tubes – there probably will not be enough light coming through the lens and the extension tube to drive the autofocusing.

Supplementary lenses and extension tubes may not be held in stock by your camera retailer or wholesaler. You might have to wait awhile before seeing them.

Using depth-of-field

With macro photography you must know how to make use of depth-of-field effectively for good results. A depth-of-field preview button is extremely helpful because it saves you a lot of guessing or referring back to tables which can be tedious and time-consuming.

Suppose, for example, you are photographing a large stick insect. As long as it is on a plane parallel to the film in your camera, focusing on it will be relatively easy and the insect's entire body should be rendered sharply on film. But if the creature decides to see what you are doing, and totters towards you like a pencil on legs, you will get little of it in focus – perhaps only its head and mouthparts.

Where you position your camera is important in macro photography. Head-on pictures of stick insects require precision focusing to begin with, and careful checking with the depth-of-field preview button to ensure that all you need is sharply represented. For example, if you focus on the insect's eyes, you may find that too much of the insect's body is blurred behind the head. Try focusing a little way down the body, and then checking to see whether the head is still needle sharp. Do this, and you

THREE IMAGES OF THE ALPINE CABBAGE TREE Cordyline indivisa

Fuji Velvia 50, Canon EOS 5 with Canon 100mm macro lens, slow shutter speeds at f/16. Tripod.
This beautiful native plant of New Zealand was photographed in Tongariro National Park during late autumn. I was attracted by the subtle colour and the lines and textures of both the mature leaves and the unfurling new ones. I used natural light, augmented by a reflector board, for the two shots of the young leaves from a smaller specimen, and fill-flash (set at - 1 on my Canon 430 EZ flashgun) and a Canon 100-300mm L zoom lens for the more brightly coloured, mature leaves, of a nearby larger specimen.

will get much more of your subject sharply in focus – it just comes with practice. Remember the smaller the aperture, the more depth-of-field you have. Note also, that the closer you get to your subject the less depth-of-field you will have available. This sad fact is simply a matter of optical geometry, and there is nothing you can do to change it.

If you have never tried macro work, I suggest that you practise coming to terms with depth-of-field by beginning with something inanimate at home – something that you can zero in on and observe the effects of changing the f/stop, while you watch what happens to your depth-of-field through the viewfinder. You'll find the exercise both valuable and absorbing.

Once you have focused on your subject and got it sharp, pay particular attention to the background. Is it desirable to have all or part of the background sharply focused, or better to have it blurred? If it's the latter option, open the lens up a stop or so, but check your focusing as you do this. You may have to refocus a little and check again before you take your picture. Do not assume that using the smallest aperture will solve all your problems. Backgrounds are very important to the composition and effectiveness of your picture, so check them carefully. And watch out for any bright objects that may detract from the subject impact, especially if they are likely to be sharp in the final picture.

Using the smallest aperture

In using a variety of lenses at their smallest aperture, I find that even the best camera light meter systems can give uneven results – most have a tendency to underexpose. You must remember that very little light is coming through the lens when it is fully stopped down – as you will see when checking the depth-of-field preview button. Moreover, because most lenses are designed to produce their best results in the middle range of apertures, f/32 can really strain both their resolution and contrast. For these reasons, when I want maximum depth-of-field and a small aperture I prefer to back off two stops from the minimum that the lens offers (from f/32 to f/16, for instance). F/16 at one second seems to be my longstanding favourite combination when using macro lenses and 50 ISO film. Such a combination gives the lightmeter a good chance to produce a better exposure, while the lens can produce a crisper image.

For exposures longer than one second, your film usually wants more light than your lightmeter might indicate. In these instances, it's a good idea to use +1 or +2 on the exposure compensation control. Leave the f/stop at f/16 or whatever you're using, to keep as much depth-of-field as you can, and alter the shutter speed rather than the f/stop.

Which raises another interesting point. Try putting your camera on Aperture Priority, put your lens on f/16, find a dark place and fire a test shot to see just how long your camera shutter is programmed to remain open for. My old Nikon FA shutter remained open for about one minute before its computer ran out of breath and released it. I have taken some good shots with this camera on exposure times of up to 45 seconds or so! Yes, they were well exposed, and no, the colour shift of the Fujichrome 50 ISO film wasn't nearly as bad as I had expected. Very acceptable results in fact. Remember, however, that this sort of photography gobbles up battery power, so be prepared with a back-up battery at all times. Most modern AF cameras operate down to 30 seconds, which is perfectly adequate for nearly all macro photography.

Lens hoods

Most modern AF macro lenses have deeply inset lens elements and the lens housing forms a perfectly suitable lens hood. If in doubt, always use a lens hood.

Filters

These are generally unnecessary for macro work. In most close-up situations, remove all filters as they detract from the image quality. Polarising filters can sometimes be helpful, but use them sparingly because they cut down the light falling on the film by about one to two stops, and this can limit your depth-of-field if you need to change your f/stop.

A plain matt screen

If you are planning to do a considerable amount of macro work with your manual focus camera, a plain screen is absolutely necessary. The old split-image screen available in most manual focus cameras will drive you mad.

Tripods and remote controllers

Elimination of all camera movement is absolutely essential to close-up photography, because the magnifications involved mean that any movement of camera or subject will be greatly exaggerated. Use a tripod and a cable release, and trip the shutter as carefully as you can. Autofocus SLR shutters operate electromagnetically and trip discreetly with a dull thud.

FOREST FUNGI Mycena sp.
Fujichrome 50 Professional, Nikon FA with Tokina 90mm ATX macro lens, f/16 at 15 secs. Tripod. Photo by Lynda Harper.
An exquisite example of why so many people enjoy close-up photography. This fungi is not much bigger than a pin, and required considerable patience to achieve such a result. Note the composition and the effective use of the dark background.

Some remote controllers have a two-stage mechanism for firing the camera shutter. You can either fire the shutter without any delay, or you can allow the camera's mirror to operate a couple of seconds before the shutter fires. This small delay eliminates any chance of camera shake due to the mirror operation. I recommend that you use the delayed firing with all your close-ups where this is feasible. Remote controllers are excellent for close-up photography and I suggest that you get this accessory when you buy your camera.

Reflector boards

To help lessen shadows, you can use a small reflector board made up of a piece of 16 x 12 cm white cardboard, or one covered with aluminium foil with its bright side outermost. I use this to reflect sunlight back towards the subject, which increases the light by up to 2 stops, lessens the contrast, and gives more depth-of-field. You can also use thin sheets of white polystyrene. Move the reflector board about to model the light falling on the subject and to create depth and substance. Having someone hold the reflector board can be a big help during the taking of the picture. Failing this, carry a 'bulldog' clip in your camera bag and use it to secure the reflector board to a handy object.

'Gardening'

Before you take the picture, check to ensure that nothing extraneous is in the way of a good photograph. Check for any stray blades of grass, twigs and the like – anything that can be removed easily which might otherwise disrupt the integrity of your image. We call this 'gardening'. Gardening does not mean the wholesale removal of twigs or leaves that might conceal a bird's nest, a small animal's lair, or jeopardize an animal's or plant's survival.

Natural light versus flash

Use natural lighting whenever you can. A sky with high overcast clouds is ideal because it helps reduce the contrast which is normally very strong in direct sunlight. Low contrast allows for good image detail.

Flash is not always the panacea for lighting problems. With many small things, such as plants, it is their natural beauty that we want to capture on film. The subtle shades of colour in an orchid flower, the texture of a leaf or wing, these and many other delicate nuances of life can be blasted away by the too bright light of a flashgun.

Flash brightness is not the only problem. Because the colour balance of flash is calibrated to be close to direct natural sunlight, it may be very different from the bright but diffuse light of the forest floor, producing a bright image but not one true to nature.

Using flash

Sometimes, however, a combination of dull light or a moving subject will require the use of a flash. Macro photography is unusual in that often there is too much light rather than not enough. The subject needs to be lit as naturally as possible, and flash light must be used carefully to prevent the image from appearing harshly and unnaturally lit.

Modern matrix fill-in flashguns and specially designed macro-ring flashguns are very easy to use for close-up photography. Because they tend to overlight some subjects, however, set the flash from minus 2/3 on the exposure compensation control and experiment by varying the exposure compensation a little. Check my comments in the chapter on Flash Photography.

Flash systems physically built into the camera are not suitable for macro photography, especially when they're set up on the camera's pentaprism. In such cases the flash beam does not align along the same axis as the lens, and for objects very close to the camera, the lens can actually block the light from the flash reaching some or all of the subject.

Modern AF cameras can have a number of flashguns attached to them and the camera electronics can adjust the light output of each to add up to the total light required. Some people use two small, dedicated TTL flash units attached to the camera by means of a flash bracket, or alternatively the flashguns may be tied to a tent peg or something similar, enabling each to be independently positioned at any distance required from the subject. All flash units off camera must be connected to it by the appropriate dedicated cable, unless you prefer to use open flash, in which case the gun can be fired manually while the shutter is open. Twin-flash technique is good for small fungi and plants where modelling of the light can create effective pictures. If, however, your subject is watching you, two catchlights will appear in its eyes. You may find this unnatural and wish to avoid it.

The simple alternative is to have a single dedicated TTL flash unit attached to the camera by a coiled extension cable. This is what I use. A small flash of low power will usually be adequate, or you can use a more powerful one, provided that you can reduce its power output. After setting up your camera on the tripod and focusing on the subject, you can hand-hold the flash unit and fire it from various positions relative to the subject. You may wish to use front lighting coming from close to the camera, in which case the best place to position the flashgun is about 10 cm (4 inches) above the front of the lens and slightly to one side. This will create a well-lit subject with a minimum of shadowing.

Another approach is sidelighting, in which you 'skim' the light over the subject to highlight its texture. This is simple to do when handholding the flash. Try different ways of using your flash, and keep notes on what you have done. In this way you will soon find a technique you prefer. Experiment, and always bracket your exposures. This is easy to do with most flashguns currently available for AF cameras.

THE ELVEN WATERFALL
Fujichrome 50 Professional, Nikon FA with Tokina ATX 90-mm macro lens, f/16 at 9 secs. Tripod.
A delicate waterfall which is no more than a metre from top to bottom and forms a small section of a large stream-bed.
A week of heavy rain later scoured out the water course and destroyed this waterfall. The elves plan to rebuild it.
Most photographers think waterfalls need to be big to be impressive. Creative photographers know better.

HERE'S LOOKING AT YOU

Fujichrome 100, Nikon F4 with Nikkor 80-200mm zoom and fill-flash with SB 24. Hand held at 200mm. f/2.8 at 1/60 sec. Photo by Paul Kennedy.

Fill-flash can spice up an ordinary shot of a raven into something special. You might try setting yourself a project to do nothing but use fill-flash for a day. Not only will you be surprised just how easy it is to use, but the results might also refresh your approach to photography.

Manual exposure mode

This leaves all the decisions up to you and is likely to be most useful for special effects.

Flash exposure compensation

If you wish to overrule what the camera or flash wants to do, you can either use the flash gun's controls or the compensation dial on the camera. The effects are additive: you could set the flash to minus 1 and camera to minus 2 to get total exposure compensation of minus 3. This can be great fun for experienced photographers, but for beginners it can get confusing. For the sake of simplicity I suggest you stay with the flash's compensation, otherwise you might forget to return the camera's compensation controls back to zero when your flash shots are finished. Although modern cameras will let you know when the exposure compensation is in use by showing the (+/–) sign it's one of those electronic reminders that seem fatefully easy to overlook.

Notes

1. I have used Nikon flashguns on matrix fill-in flash as described above, but I find the flash light produced can be a bit too bright for my liking. To counter this, I reduce the flash output by bringing up the flash's exposure compensation display, and reducing the flash output as follows.

For front ambient lighting, reduce the flash output by **minus 2 stops**.

For side ambient lighting, reduce the flash output by **minus 1.5 stops**.

For backlighting, **leave the flash uncompensated.**

I would suggest that you run a test film using the matrix exactly as the camera wants you to, and experiment by reducing the flash output as described above. After having made careful notes in your photographic logbook while you're doing this, you will be able to check all three results. Watch out for unwelcome double shadows that too much flash light might provide you with and make sure that your subject is within the range of your flash – do this by checking the distance scale on the back of the flash: this can change automatically whenever you reset the flash.

2. I have also found that the light from the Canon and the Nikon flashguns can be a bit cool (the colour temperature) for my liking. You can warm it up by either placing an amber gel on the flash unit or by adding an amber filter to your lens. Try a few test shots with and without the filters and check your results.

Slow Synchronization Flash

Most automatic flashguns will synchronize with a shutter speed between 1/250 and 1/60 of a second, which is too fast to allow the dim background light on to your film. The result is a black background – your flower looks as if it has been photographed at midnight. To avoid this we can use Slow Synchronization Flash. Here the camera reads the existing light levels as, say, 1 second at f/16 and takes the picture at this setting – but adds just enough flash light to fill in the details and illuminate the subject properly. Very clever. Try flash compensation settings just in case the flash light turns out to be a bit too strong. I generally use a minus 1 or minus 2 compensation in this situation. Whatever you do, write your results in your photographic logbook and check the results carefully.

'Rear curtain flash'

Rear curtain fill-in matrix flash isn't a rare tropical disease but is a very handy creative device for nature photographers.

Suppose your subject is a group of rare alpine flowers nodding about in a summer breeze. What to do? The flowers won't look this lovely next week and you're deep in a National Park where someone might object if you're tempted to remove them for a portrait at your place rather than on the mountain. The light might be satisfactory, but at f/16 the shutter speed will definitely be too slow to prevent blurring. Try rear-curtain flash. While the shutter is open, the flowers will continue to bob about, but when the flash fires, you should get a soft blurring of the flowers generated by the natural light, and a perfectly exposed, sharply focused group of flowers stopped in their tracks by the split second, main light of the flashlight. Try it and see.

Rear-curtain flash is easiest to use on Aperture Priority.

How important is the shutter speed in flash photography?

Not much, unless you are doing a large number of slow speed, fill-in flash shots. Modern cameras will usually switch over automatically to the correct synchronized shutter speed if you have left your shutter setting in the wrong place. As long as the flash can deliver all its computed light on to the film while the shutter is open, (which it does exceedingly quickly – to about 1/20,000th of a second) depending on how far away your subject is, the shutter speed is almost irrelevant. The camera shutter speed could actually be anywhere from 30 seconds to the maximum synchronized flash speed – currently about 1/250 of a second.

How important is the f/stop?

Very. Always check the f/stop for your nature flash shots. For my macro shots I use f/16, TTL matrix fill-in flash on -1 or -2 , and rear curtain flash. There will be times when you will want to use a larger opening to isolate your subject from its background. Remember, too, that if your subject is white you may need minus 2 or minus 3 to light it appropriately without overexposing it with too much light from the flash.

Flash battery duration

Modern flash units recycle in a matter of moments, providing up to 100 flashes before their batteries need replacing. The more powerful the flash, and the further the light has to travel in order to illuminate the subject, the more quickly the batteries will be used up. Always carry spare batteries.

Buying a flash unit

Stay with the same brand for both camera and flash. Not to do so is inviting all sorts of annoying and potentially disastrous incompatibilities.

Flash unit failure

Flash units normally fail to work because of run-down batteries. Make sure your batteries are fresh and always carry a spare set. Be careful of rechargeable Ni-Cad batteries as these often do not have the correct voltage, and can fail to charge up the flashgun for firing. The result is a long anxious wait, with no flash at the end of it.

FIORDLAND CRESTED PENGUINS ***Eudyptes pachyrhynchus*** *MEET MODERN TECHNOLOGY*

Fujichrome 100 Professional, Canon EOS 10 with Sigma 75-300mm APO zoom lens and Canon 430 EZ dedicated fill flash. Camera set on Program auto flash: distance 2.5 meters at f/8.

This species, the world's rarest penguin, nests along the wet isolated shores of south-western New Zealand. I photographed this pair inside a dark sea cave, using the flash as the sole means of illumination. Because the entire scene was so dark, I compensated the flash output to overexpose by one stop in order to achieve the result shown here. The small infra-red beam emitted by the camera for autofocusing briefly lit up the cave with an ethereal glow but allowed the lens to focus on the penguins quickly and easily. Penguins can't detect infra-red light, but they certainly saw the main flash. It didn't seem to worry them much – they remained comfortably seated, where they were, until we left.

Remove batteries from your flash when storing it, and make sure you wipe the terminals clean on the batteries themselves and in the flashgun housing when refitting. The small eraser at the end of a pencil is ideal for this task. Batteries will often 'sweat' over a period of time, and the resulting acidic moisture can lead to electrical shorts and corrosion. Never mix old and new batteries. I write the purchase date on mine to help avoid this.

Shooting them in the eye

If you fire a flash directly at an animal in darkness, the light will pass through the wide-open pupil of the eye and return to the film showing the blood-red retina at the back of the animal's eyes. This condition is called *red-eye* , and it looks rather unearthly; it certainly destroys a natural image. Some flash units overcome this by firing one or more small pre-flash beams which reduces the pupil of the subject's eyes before the main flash fires. Another way to avoid this is to place the flash off to the side of the camera, or provide other lighting that reduces the size of the subject's pupils.

The camera's accessory shoe

A flash unit built into the top of the camera is not really suitable for nature photography, as I have already mentioned in the preceding chapter on Close-up Photography. Moreover, I never use a flash attached to the camera accessory shoe. Indeed, I wish camera makers would leave them off the camera. Because a camera necessarily looks directly at its subject, any flash on the camera must do the same thing. The resulting light tends to be hard and flat and lacks anything resembling natural shadowing. This is perfectly acceptable for relatively flat surfaces, such as crustose lichens on rocks, but not for most other nature photography.

Extension cables

Buy an expanding dedicated extension cable which allows you to take your flash off the camera, but make sure it preserves the full flash metering facilities of your camera. Such cables are not cheap but are well worth having. By separating flash and camera, shadows are created on the side opposite the light source, and this gives an appearance of roundness and form to your subject.

How many flash units should you have?

As many as you like. You can connect several dedicated flashguns together using the appropriate cables and leave the camera's computer to work out the correct exposure. I prefer just one – off camera and connected to it with a dedicated cable.

Macro ring flashes

These fit snugly around a macro lens and use twin flash tubes mounted on either side on the lens. The earlier criticism of them was that they gave very flat – no shadow – lighting, but the newer ring flashes allow you to fire either the right or left of the twin flashes, thus providing a bit of shadow moulding to your subject. Because they can be rotated, you can control the placement and angle of shadows in your photograph. Use Aperture Control or Manual Exposure for best results.

Macro Ring flashes that I have seen recently do not have the facility to reduce their output independently from that of the camera, which could be a nuisance if you want to alter the relationship between the camera's meter reading for the ambient light levels and the amount of light generated by the flash. In other words, you can't use exposure compensation with Macro Ring flashes as you can with the modern, dedicated flashguns. This manufacturing glitch will probably be attended to soon.

Photographing animals at night

Animals at night require either one powerful flashgun or several guns hooked together. To locate animals, wildlife photographers often use battery powered lights attached to their heads with elastic head bands. These are excellent, provided they are carefully positioned to shine directly in front of you and slightly downwards. Such lights allow both hands to be free for your camera. An alternative is to strap a torch on to the top of your telephoto lens, using a couple of elastic bands.

If the animal is some distance away, wait a few seconds longer after the 'ready' light appears in the viewfinder. Ready lights usually become visible when the flash is only about 80 per cent charged and not at full power. For animals at night, open up the lens an extra two stops.

Freezing the action

Electronic flashes discharge at superfast speeds. 'Computer' flashes may have a flash duration of from 1/400 second to 1/40,000 second, depending on how close the subject is. The closer the subject, the shorter the flash duration. Regardless of what shutter speed you are using, the flash effectively freezes all movement, and can be useful when photographing small birds flying on to the edge of their nest, or for freezing the motion of falling water. By taking advantage of this high speed flash photography, you will be able to examine things that could otherwise never be stopped in their tracks.

Parting remarks

Modern AF cameras and their companion flash units make taking flash shots of nature a relatively simple matter. Read your instruction book carefully. Don't leave your flash at home just because it's a bright sunshiny day. Take it. Use it, for things like fill-in flash and for freezing fast action. AF flash is one of the most creative and interesting tools that we have at our disposal.

TUI DE ROY PHOTOGRAPHING HAWKS ON THE GALAPAGOS ISLANDS
We began with a photograph of a jackdaw over Nepal. We finish with alighting Galapagos hawks at the Galapagos Islands. Nature photography offers us endless paths to creative enjoyment. Good luck, and safe journeys.

Whatever your photograph, do it right. Look, plan, and consider before you shoot. Remember the three rules of good composition: simplify; simplify; simplify. A good picture that is easy to read is far more evocative than words.

Learn how to walk away from an indifferent shot. Be creative. Seek a better way of photographing what you see.

Don't take your photography too seriously, and don't be too protective of your work. Always be ready to do better next time.

And at the risk of my repeating myself: Enjoy nature photography for what it is: an absorbing journey to self discovery.

Adams, Ansel. 1974. *Images 1923-1974.* New York Graphic Society, Boston, (Mass.).

Alinder, James, Szarkowski, J. 1985. *Ansel Adams: Classic Images.* New York Graphic Society, Boston (Mass.).

Andrews, Gordon. 1987. *Seeing.* Craftman House, Seaforth, Australia.

Bishop, Nic. 1989. *Untouched Horizons.* Hodder & Stoughton. Auckland, London, Sydney.

Dalton, Stephen. 1988. *Secret Lives.* Century. London, Melbourne, Auckland.

Deichmann, G. & Cope,T. 1989. *Northern Images: Australia's Northern Territory.* Collins, Australia.

Godwin, Fay. 1985. *Land.* William Heinemann, London and Auckland.

Haas, Ernst. 1988. *The Creation.* Penguin Books, New York, London.

Harper, Peter. 1989. *Photographing Nature.* The Caxton Press, Christchurch, New Zealand.

Kampion, Drew, 1989. *The Book of Waves.* Appel Books, Colorado.

Kunkel, Reinhard, 1992. *Ngorongoro.* Harvill, London.

Lehrman, F. 1988. *The Sacred Landscape.* Celestial Arts, Berkerley California.

Maeda, Shinzo 1986. *Hills of Color: Scenes and Seasons.* Graphic-sha Publishing Co. Tokyo, Japan.

Maeda, Shinzo 1986. *A Tree, A Blade of Grass.* Graphic-sha Publishing Co. Tokyo, Japan.

McBride, S. 1989. *The Spirit of England.* Webb & Bower/Michael Joseph, London.

Monteath, C, et al. 1990. *Wild Ice. Antarctic Journeys.* Smithsonian Institution, Washington, D.C., United States.

Patterson, Freeman. 1985. *Photography and the art of seeing.* Key Porter. Toronto, Canada.

Patterson, Freeman. 1987. *Portraits of Earth.* Key Porter. Toronto, Canada.

Porter, Eliot. & Glick, James. 1990. *Natures Chaos.* Viking Penguin, New York, London, Auckland.

Rowell, Galen. 1986. *Mountain light. In search of the dynamic landscape.* Century Hutchinson, Auckland and London.

Sexton, John. 1990. *Quiet Light.* Bulfinch Press. Little, Brown and Company, Boston, Toronto, London.

Shaw, John. 1984. *The nature photographer's complete guide to professional field techniques.* Amphoto, New York.

Shaw, John. 1992. *Focus on Nature.* Harper Collins, London.

Wolfe, Art. & Davidson, A. 1990. *Alakshak: The Great Country.* Sierra Club Books, San Francisco.